MONOGRAPHS OF THE SOCIETY FOR RESEARCH IN CHILD DEVELOPMENT

SERIAL NO. 221, VOL. 55, NOS. 1–2, 1990

CONTEXTS OF ACHIEVEMENT: A STUDY OF AMERICAN, CHINESE, AND JAPANESE CHILDREN

HAROLD W. STEVENSON
SHIN-YING LEE

IN COLLABORATION WITH
CHUANSHENG CHEN
JAMES W. STIGLER
CHEN-CHIN HSU
SEIRO KITAMURA

WITH COMMENTARY BY
GIYOO HATANO

AND A REPLY BY THE AUTHORS

MONOGRAPHS OF THE SOCIETY FOR RESEARCH IN CHILD DEVELOPMENT, SERIAL NO. 221, VOL. 55, NOS. 1–2, 1990

CONTENTS

Abstract	v
I. Introduction	1
II. Research Procedures	8
III. Achievement in Reading and Mathematics	18
IV. Background Information: Schools and Teachers	29
V. Background Information: Families and Children	36
VI. Children's Lives at Home	42
VII. Children's Attitudes	49
VIII. Beliefs about Effort and Ability	59
IX. Mothers' Evaluations of Their Child's Cognitive Abilities, School Performance, Motivation, and Personality	68
X. Mothers' Satisfaction with Their Child's School Performance and Evaluations of Curriculum and School	76
XI. Problems in Schooling according to Mothers and Teachers	83
XII. Discussion	94
References	104
Acknowledgments	107

COMMENTARY

Toward the Cultural Psychology of Mathematical Cognition, By Giyoo Hatano	108

REPLY

TO ACHIEVE,
BY HAROLD W. STEVENSON AND SHIN-YING LEE   116

CONTRIBUTORS   120

ABSTRACT

STEVENSON, HAROLD W., and LEE, SHIN-YING, in collaboration with CHEN, CHUANSHENG; STIGLER, JAMES W.; HSU, CHEN-CHIN; and KITAMURA, SEIRO. Contexts of Achievement: A Study of American, Chinese, and Japanese Children. With Commentary by GIYOO HATANO; and a Reply by HAROLD W. STEVENSON and SHIN-YING LEE. *Monographs of the Society for Research in Child Development*, 1990, **55**(1–2, Serial No. 221).

The major purpose of this study was to attempt to understand some of the reasons for the high academic achievement of Chinese and Japanese children compared to American children. The study was conducted with first and fifth graders attending elementary schools in the Minneapolis metropolitan area, Taipei (Taiwan), and Sendai (Japan). 1,440 children (240 first graders and 240 fifth graders in each city) were selected as target subjects in the study. The children were selected from 20 classrooms at each grade in each city and constituted a representative sample of children from these classrooms. In a follow-up study, first graders were studied again when they were in the fifth grade.

The children were tested with achievement tests in reading and mathematics constructed specifically for this study, the children and their mothers were interviewed, the children's teachers filled out a questionnaire, and interviews were held with the principals of the schools attended by the children. In the follow-up study, achievement tests were administered, and the children and their mothers were interviewed.

Background information about the children's everyday lives revealed much greater attention to academic activities among Chinese and Japanese than among American children. Members of the three cultures differed significantly in terms of parents' interest in their child's academic achievement, involvement of the family in the child's education, standards and expectations of parents concerning their child's academic achievement, and parents' and children's beliefs about the relative influence of effort and ability on academic achievement. Whereas children's academic achievement did not appear to be a central concern of American mothers, Chinese and Japanese mothers viewed this as their child's most important pursuit. Once the child entered elementary school, Chinese and Japanese families mobilized themselves to assist the child and to provide an environment conducive to achievement. American mothers appeared to be less interested in their child's academic achievement than in the child's general cognitive development; they attempted to provide experiences that fostered cognitive growth rather than academic excellence. Chinese and Japanese mothers held higher standards for their children's achievement than American mothers and gave more realistic evaluations of their child's academic, cognitive, and personality characteristics. American mothers overestimated their child's abilities and expressed greater satisfaction with their child's accomplishments than the Chinese and Japanese mothers. In describing bases of children's academic achievement, Chinese and Japanese mothers stressed the importance of hard work to a greater degree than American mothers, and American mothers gave greater emphasis to innate ability than did Chinese and Japanese mothers.

I. INTRODUCTION

Poor performance by American students on tests of mathematics and science has reached the level of a national crisis. Study after study has reported on one or another facet of the low standing of Americans in international competition. For example, in a recent cross-national study of mathematics achievement, American students in the eighth and twelfth grades were below the international average in problem solving, geometry, algebra, calculus, and other areas of mathematics. In contrast, Japanese eighth graders received the highest average scores of children from 20 countries, and, at the twelfth-grade level, Japanese students were second only to Chinese students in Hong Kong (Garden, 1987; McKnight et al., 1987). Similar results have been reported in cross-national comparisons of achievement in science (e.g., Comber & Keeves, 1973). We must ask why this is the case. Why are Chinese and Japanese students consistently among the top scorers in cross-national studies of achievement and American students consistently below the international average? The primary purpose of this research project was to attempt to provide some answers to this question. All the prior studies compared the performance of middle and high school students in different countries. We were interested in exploring cross-cultural differences in academic achievement of younger children. Our first major concern was to determine whether there are cross-cultural differences in academic achievement during elementary school that anticipate those that have been documented among older students. Our second major concern was to describe the contexts in which different levels of achievement occur in these three cultures. We sought to identify not only contexts that appear to be important in explaining differences that we observed at the early years but also those that might be related to the cross-cultural differences in achievement that have been found among older children and youths.

Recent discussions of academic achievement of Asians have centered on Japan, primarily because the academic performance of children has been considered in the context of the remarkable economic development that has occurred in that country during the past several decades. Westerners want to understand why Japan has been successful both in the classroom and in the marketplace. More recently, economic and political changes taking place in Taiwan have stimulated an increased interest in Taiwan as well. Explanations of the economic development in both Japan and Taiwan often attribute their success to an intensely dedicated, well-educated work force (e.g., Christopher, 1983; Vogel, 1979). An examination of educational practices and of cultural factors that underlie them should help to clarify how such a well-educated work force has been created.

There have been numerous descriptions of the education of Japanese children (e.g., Cummings, 1980; De Vos, 1973; Duke, 1986; Lebra & Lebra, 1974; Lewis, 1984; Lynn, 1988; Rohlen, 1983; Stevenson, Azuma, & Hakuta, 1986; and White, 1987), but there is little information about psychological or cultural factors associated with the education of Chinese children. Wilson's (1970) early book and the more recent books by Kessen (1975), Munro (1977), and Bond (1986) are among the few that consider broad issues in Chinese children's development and education. In all cases, descriptions of both Japanese and Chinese education have relied on observations made during visits to schools, or on conversations with parents, teachers, and school officials, rather than on formal studies yielding data amenable to statistical analysis. Informal observations made by astute observers are informative, but there is always the possibility of bias and misinterpretation. There is a great need for data obtained under more controlled conditions.

Rather than study older students, we chose elementary school children as our subjects for several reasons. First, we wanted to know if cross-cultural differences in achievement emerged during these early years of schooling and especially whether they were evident as early as the first grade. If this proved to be the case, it would be difficult to account for cross-cultural differences in achievement primarily in terms of the educational practices of the schools. A second reason for focusing on elementary school children was to gain some understanding of the early antecedents of the large differences that appear later in middle and senior high school.

There is a paucity, too, of comparative studies in which the practices of Chinese and Japanese parents and teachers have been compared with those found in other societies. A notable exception is the longitudinal research of Azuma, Hess, and Kashiwagi, who followed two groups of children, one in Tokyo and one in the Bay Area of California, from the time they were in preschool through their elementary school years. Numerous publications from this study have appeared both in Japanese (e.g., Azuma, Kashiwagi, & Hess, 1981) and in English (e.g., Hess, Holloway, Dickson, & Price, 1984).

Educators and social scientists have long been interested in describing the contexts of academic achievement, and each discipline has approached the task in very different ways. Educators have concentrated on the school, its organization, teaching practices, the curriculum, and classroom life (e.g., Goodlad, 1984). Sociologists have been more likely to examine such factors as the influence of socioeconomic and ethnic status, parents' education, age, sex, and other demographic variables (e.g., Coleman et al., 1966). Psychologists have typically investigated the influence of such variables as intelligence, personality, motivation, and cognitive functions on school performance (e.g., Paris, Olson, & Stevenson, 1983). Others, such as Entwisle, have successfully combined several approaches (e.g., Entwisle & Hayduk, 1978).

Ours was a broad, exploratory study in which we included as many different methods as possible. In addition to studying the children's achievement in reading and mathematics, we tested their cognitive abilities, observed them and their teachers in classrooms, and interviewed the children as well as their parents and teachers. Four years after completing the initial study, we conducted a follow-up of the first graders when they were in the fifth grade in order to chart their progress through elementary school and to obtain additional information about their lives from them and from their mothers.

To evaluate the children's academic achievement, we needed measures that could be used in the three cultures. Rather than relying on translations of existing tests whose relevance to the children's academic experiences varied across countries, we decided to develop our own tests in reading and mathematics based on detailed analyses of the textbooks used in the locations where the study was conducted.

This was a large study, and some of our findings—such as the reports of our classroom observations and the results of our cognitive tests given to the children—have been published (Stevenson et al., 1985; Stevenson et al., 1987; Stigler, Lee, & Stevenson, 1987). We refer to these reports at times, but complete information can be obtained in the original reports.

The major source of information for the present report came from the interviews. Nearly 1,500 first- and fifth-grade children and their mothers, carefully selected to constitute representative samples from three large metropolitan areas in Taiwan, Japan, and the United States, participated in the study. We regret that interviews with fathers could not be arranged. Because it was not feasible to obtain a national sample of subjects, we were forced to select a single metropolitan area to represent each culture. Our generalizations are thereby limited to the degree that these cities fail to represent each culture.

The interviews were wide ranging and contained both objective and open-ended questions. We obtained background information on demographic characteristics of the family, the home environment, and the children's experiences before they entered school. Although our primary interest was in children's lives outside the elementary school classrooms, we also needed to learn how school life impinged on home life. Questions were asked about contacts between parents and teachers, the daily schedule in school, the curricula, characteristics of the teachers, and problems related to education that were encountered by the children, parents, and teachers. Questions about parents' involvement in their child's education and the child's after-school educational activities also were included.

Parents' perceptions of their child's capabilities are an important factor in their expectations for that child. Thus, we asked each mother to rate her child on a number of academic, cognitive, and personality characteristics. Regardless of a mother's assessments of her child's capabilities, she may or may not be satisfied with what the child is accomplishing. Several approaches were taken to determine mothers' satisfaction with their child's performance and how they and their child explained success and failure.

We believe that a thorough understanding of the strengths and weaknesses of the American educational system is possible only through the perspectives provided by comparative data. Chinese and Japanese societies, in particular, provide important cases for comparison because the educational achievement of their children and youths has been so outstanding. By providing comparative data for large, representative samples of children, mothers, and teachers in Taipei (Taiwan), Sendai (Japan), and Minneapolis (the United States), the present study makes a potentially important contribution to our understanding of child development and education in these three cultures.

GENERAL FACTORS UNDERLYING ACHIEVEMENT

Logically, children's academic achievement is related to three major factors: their intelligence, their experiences at school, and their experiences at home. With regard to the first factor, it seems unlikely that cross-national differences in academic achievement among Chinese, Japanese, and American children can be accounted for by differences in general intelligence. There is no evidence that Chinese and Japanese children are more intelligent than American children. A widely quoted study that reported differences between the IQs of Japanese and American children (Lynn, 1982) has been shown to be problematic on the grounds that the samples in the two countries were not comparable in terms of urban-rural and socioeconomic background—two variables significantly related to scores on intelligence tests (Stevenson & Azuma, 1983). When comparability in backgrounds is assured and children are tested with culturally appropriate materials, differences in general level of intellectual functioning between Japanese, Chinese, and American children have not been found (Stevenson et al., 1985). We gave the children who served as subjects in the present study a battery of 10 cognitive tasks constructed expressly for the research. The tasks were typical of those contained in intelligence tests and included tests of vocabulary, general information, digit span, verbal memory, spatial relations, perceptual speed, auditory memory, coding, verbal-spatial representation, and serial memory for words. An overall score from all the tests was constructed, and by fifth grade there were no differences in the mean of these scores for the children from the three cultures. Differences did appear on the individual tests, but these were unsystematic. For example, Sendai children received higher scores than children in Minneapolis and Taipei did on spatial relations, but the Chinese children exceeded the American and the Japanese children on coding; Minneapolis children received higher scores on verbal memory than children in Sendai and higher scores than Taipei children on perceptual speed. Positing differences in cognitive functioning to explain the superior academic achievement of Chinese and Japanese children may be appealing, but these data and similar findings reported by Lynn and Hampson (1986) fail to provide any support for such a hypothesis.

Chinese, Japanese, and American children do have very different experiences at school. This is immediately evident to anyone who has visited schools in these cultures, looked at the children's textbooks, or read ethnographic analyses of classroom practices. The school environment is the first general context for academic achievement that we explore here. These explorations rely heavily on our interviews with the teachers and principals and to some extent on the results of the observational study we conducted. Because the results of the latter have already been published (Stevenson et al., 1987; Stigler et al., 1987), we use these data selectively.

The second major context for children's academic achievement is their everyday experiences outside of school. It is this context to which we direct our main attention in this report. Information about the children's lives at home came from interviews we conducted with the children and their mothers. Of central interest were cultural differences in beliefs, attitudes, and expectations, especially those related to schoolwork.

THEMES OF THE STUDY

We did not develop specific prior hypotheses because information from previous work was insufficient to allow us to be confident about our characterizations of each culture. As we indicated earlier, there is an enormous literature in the social sciences concerning the correlates of academic achievement, but it is predominantly the product of research conducted in the United States and Western Europe. Although it was not our purpose to evaluate the usefulness of the constructs that have emerged from this work in explaining differences in achievement in the three cultures at issue, we did use them to help us in organizing some of our interview material. In addition to obtaining demographic data and information about the parents and about the children's experiences before entering school, most of the remaining questions were organized around the following five themes.

1. *Emphasis on academic achievement.*—Children's academic achievement is given a more central role in some cultures than in others. In developing countries such as Taiwan, personal advancement is closely linked to academic achievement, and there is great emphasis on education. In Japan, where natural resources are limited, progress in technology and science is essential for the nation's economic health, and such progress is highly dependent on having a well-educated work force. Other cultures have different goals. Some value experiences that stimulate children to think and build up a broad fund of knowledge, regardless of whether such experiences result in higher school grades; others stress the importance of children's developing a sense of self-worth. The goal of education in these societies is not only the acquisition of specific types of knowledge but also the development of children who feel good about themselves and their capabilities; self-confidence is believed to facilitate later learning. In other words, while some cultures value activities that help a child master prescribed skills, others, such as that in the United States, value experiences that will make a child more creative and confident.

2. *Emphasis on group participation.*—The degree to which parents, family, and other members of society become involved in children's development and education is likely to differ, depending on the society's conception of the individual in relation to these entities. The firmness of boundaries separating individual, family, and group has important implications for children's development. In some cultures, such as that in the United States, the individual is deemed to be responsible for his or her accomplishments and difficulties; in others, such as the Chinese and Japanese cultures, members of the family, teachers, or a larger group—such as pupils in the same classroom—are expected to assume some of the responsibility. As the interdependence among individuals increases, their mutual obligations to each other also increase. Individuals in such situations work hard not only to satisfy their own goals but also to meet the goals set by their families and teachers, and the success of the group is valued as highly as the success of particular individuals within the group.

3. *Realism in evaluation.*—We know that individuals differ in how realistically they evaluate their own and others' skills and potentialities; it seems reasonable to posit that cultures also differ in this respect. In studies of parental evaluations of children's capabilities, the closer the match between parental evaluations and the child's ability, the better the developmental outcome (e.g., Miller, 1988). Parents whose views are realistic are more likely to adapt interactions with their child to a level appropriate to the child's abilities than are parents who overestimate or underestimate what their

child is capable of doing. The same effect would be expected at the societal level: members of some societies may generally be realistic in evaluating themselves and their children, and others may be biased and give excessively favorable or unfavorable ratings. Realistic evaluation should create the more positive environment for academic achievement.

4. *Standards of performance.*—Closely related to the realism with which members of a society evaluate the child's and their own performance are the societal standards for performance. There is a range within which the match between actual performance and external standards is optimal for continued improvement. Individuals have little motivation for increasing their effort if standards are too low; if standards are too high, however, feelings of frustration and hopelessness are likely to develop. Information about the standards for achievement that operate within a culture is critical for understanding motivation for achievement.

5. *Effort and ability.*—The existence of differences in innate ability is widely acknowledged, but the emphasis placed on this factor relative to the influence of experience varies greatly among cultures. Some cultures deemphasize its contribution to achievement, concentrating instead on the role of hard work and effort; any limitations on achievement are attributed to a lack of diligence on the part of the learner. This is in marked contrast with cultures holding the stronger nativistic view that not all children are capable of the same levels of achievement, no matter how hard they work.

The greater the cultural emphasis on effort, the more likely it is that parents and teachers will believe that they can be instrumental in aiding children in their academic achievement. This belief is transmitted to children, and they, too, come to believe that diligence will lead to success. If, however, adults believe that innate ability imposes critical limitations on children's progress in school, it seems unlikely that they would be motivated to make such strong efforts at assistance. Japan and Taiwan, like other countries influenced by the Confucian belief in human malleability, are among the cultures that place great weight on the possibility of advancement through effort.

The ways in which these particular questions were related to these themes will be evident in the discussion of results. We begin, however, with an overview of the procedures used in the study.

II. RESEARCH PROCEDURES

RESEARCH SITES

Minneapolis.—We selected the Minneapolis metropolitan area as the site of our research in the United States. Many factors were considered in our choice of an American city; among the most important was its ethnic and racial composition. Selecting a city with a diverse ethnic population would require inclusion of ethnic status as a variable in all our analyses. This would have made it necessary to reduce the number of subjects in each ethnic group below what we believed to be desirable. Minneapolis residents tend to come from native-born, English-speaking families. These factors, we assumed, would provide an advantageous linguistic and cultural environment for learning reading and mathematics. If children's achievement in Minneapolis compared unfavorably with that of the Japanese and Chinese children, we assumed that even less favorable comparisons would be found in other cities in the United States where greater proportions of children speak English as a second language, come from economically disadvantaged homes, and have parents whose cultural backgrounds diverge from the typical middle-class milieu to which American elementary school curricula are addressed.

Approximately 2 million people live in the Minneapolis–St. Paul metropolitan area—nearly half the total population of the state of Minnesota. Minneapolis is a commercial center for a large region of the Upper Midwest, with a diverse economic base including electronics, milling, machinery manufacturing, and food processing.

The Minneapolis metropolitan area contains 16 independent school districts, a parochial school system, and 28 private schools. The total elementary school enrollment is approximately 85,000 children. The 10 schools selected for study were sampled from among school systems throughout this metropolitan area.

Taipei (Taiwan).—Taipei was chosen primarily because it was the largest Chinese city in which such research could be conducted at the time we began our project. (Hong Kong was considered, but rejected, because it has been so strongly influenced by Western culture.) Although several dialects of Chinese are spoken in Taipei, instruction in schools is conducted in Mandarin Chinese, the national language.

The population of Taiwan is approximately 19 million, of which nearly 2.5 million reside in the Taipei metropolitan area. A modern industrial city whose residents have attained a relatively high standard of living and broad educational opportunities, Taipei represents a blend of both modern and traditional cultures and is the major administrative and commercial city in Taiwan. The population of Taiwan consists primarily of two major groups, those who migrated from mainland China several centuries ago and those who left mainland China in 1949.

The organization of schools in Taiwan is similar to that in the United States. Children enter school in September after their sixth birthday, and attendance is compulsory through the ninth grade. As in the United States, over 99% of 6-year-olds attend elementary schools to which they are assigned according to the district within which they reside. In Taipei, 136 elementary schools provide education for approximately 290,000 children; the range in terms of socioeconomic status of the families and educational level of the parents included within each school district is much greater than in the United States. Approximately one-third of the children in our Taipei sample had attended preschool, and a high percentage (81%) of the children had spent at least 1 year in kindergarten (*youzhiyuan*). Admission to levels of education beyond the ninth grade in Taiwan is by competitive examination.

Sendai (Japan).—We chose Sendai for two reasons. First, it is a more traditional Japanese city than cities near Tokyo, which have been strongly influenced by the West. Second, from our own observations and from the opinions of individuals who know both Japan and the United States, it is the city in Japan that has a cultural and economic status most similar to that of Minneapolis in the United States.

Sendai is 350 kilometers northeast of Tokyo, in the Tohoku region. It has a metropolitan population of 665,000, and, including the suburbs, its total population is approximately 1.22 million persons. Most of the industry in Sendai consists of small or medium-sized enterprises; 99% employ fewer than 100 persons. The city was devastated by air raids in 1945, and much of its central part has been rebuilt since that time.

Universal public education is provided by 80 elementary schools that enroll approximately 60,000 children. Children enter school at the age of 6 years after spending a year or more in kindergarten (*yochien*). In Sendai, 98% of the 6-year-olds attended kindergarten, a percentage similar to that for 6-year-olds in the United States. Children spend 6 years in elementary school, followed by 3 years in middle school and 3 years in high school.

MONOGRAPHS

Admission to university is through competitive entrance examinations. Unlike Minneapolis and Taipei, where the school year begins in September and ends in early summer, the school year in Sendai begins in April and continues, with several holidays, until the middle of March of the following year.

WRITTEN LANGUAGES

Learning to read Chinese, a logographic writing system, and Japanese, a writing system that uses both logographs and syllabaries, is quite different from learning to read a language such as English, which is represented by a written alphabet. Brief descriptions of these writing systems will be helpful, therefore, for readers who are unfamiliar with these languages. More detailed discussions of written Chinese can be found in Lee, Ichikawa, and Stevenson (1987) and of Japanese in Stevenson et al. (1986).

Chinese.—Chinese is written solely with Chinese characters, which are best described as complex logographs, each representing a syllable of speech. Single characters generally do not represent complete words; rather, most words are composed of two or three characters. A knowledge of about 3,000 characters is necessary for reasonable literacy. The impression given in many Western descriptions of Chinese is that in learning to read Chinese the child's task is to discriminate the patterns of lines that constitute a character and then to memorize the meaning attached to the pattern. In fact, a Chinese character does not have a fixed, unitary meaning, so the same characters can have different meanings in different words. Descriptions of Chinese characters also suggest that one component ("radical") of a character reveals something about its meaning and that the other component provides information about its pronunciation. Unfortunately, the assistance obtained by analysis of these components is usually minimal because, as the writing system evolved over thousands of years, the relation between script, pronunciation, and idea has become increasingly complicated. To assist children in pronouncing characters, *zhuyin fuhao*, a phonetic spelling system in which the pronunciation of each Chinese character can be represented by no more than three of the system's 37 symbols, is used in Taiwan.

The *zhuyin fuhao* system is taught during the first semester of first grade, and, after 8–11 weeks of instruction, Chinese characters are introduced. *Zhuyin fuhao* notation continues to be printed alongside characters in the reading text for the first several years of elementary school. Several characters are taught each day, and, by the end of the sixth grade, children are able to read approximately 3,000 characters, which, in different combinations, can form many more than 3,000 words.

Japanese.—In order to read Japanese—which has been described as "certainly the most difficult system of written communication in general use in the contemporary world" (Christopher, 1983, p. 40)—two syllabaries, a system of romanization, and a subset of Chinese characters must be mastered. When only one of the syllabaries is used, reading is easy. For example, in *hiragana*, the more commonly used syllabary, each of 46 symbols corresponds to a distinct syllable. Once the symbol is learned, anything written in *hiragana* can be read; however, except for books for young children, practically nothing is written solely in *hiragana*. The other syllabary, *katakana*, contains the same sounds represented in *hiragana* but is used primarily for foreign words that have been incorporated into the Japanese language. Some words or abbreviations, such as those used in the metric system, appear in children's books in romanized form (*romaji*). *Kanji*, Chinese characters used singly or in combination to represent words, are a critical component of written Japanese. Imported from China many hundreds of years ago, these characters were given Japanese pronunciations, and their Chinese pronunciations were incorporated into the Japanese language. Consequently, nearly every character in written Japanese has both a Japanese (*kun*) and a Chinese (*on*) pronunciation. Moreover, Japanese does not make use of tones that distinguish the pronunciation of different characters in Chinese and hence contains a large number of characters with the same pronunciation. The existence of single characters with multiple pronunciations, and of multiple characters with single pronunciations, adds to the difficulty of learning to read Japanese.

By the end of the second half of the first grade, the Japanese child is presented with sentences that include three of the forms of writing—*hiragana, katakana,* and *kanji*. During the first grade of the Japanese elementary school curriculum, 46 *kanji* are taught; in the next five grades, over 900 more are added. By the end of middle school, all students are expected to be able to read a minimum of 1,850 *kanji* that are considered to be necessary for the literate person.

COUNTING SYSTEMS

Although Chinese and Japanese notations of numerical quantity employ the same Arabic numerals that are used in English, their pronunciation systems differ in that the Chinese and Japanese spoken numeral corresponds directly with the base 10 system of numeration. Thus, for example, in both Chinese and Japanese, the pronunciation of "3,246" is "three-thousands, two-hundreds, four-tens, six." The importance of this representational system for facility with number concepts by young children has been pointed out by Miura, Kim, Chang, and Okamoto (1988), and it may be a factor contributing to differences in mathematics achievement of young Asian and non-Asian children.

SUBJECTS

We were faced with two alternatives for selecting subjects: we could either choose a random sample of children from all schools in each metropolitan area or select a representative sample of schools in each city and then randomly select samples of children from these schools. We chose the second alternative as the more practical approach. Representative samples of schools were chosen on the basis of advice from educational authorities in each city. Lists of schools stratified by region, socioeconomic status of the families, and source of funding (public or private) were obtained. We then selected 10 schools to constitute a representative sample within each city. From each school, we randomly selected two grade 1 and two grade 5 classrooms. Because not all the 10 Minneapolis schools had two first- or two fifth-grade classrooms, three additional schools were included to yield the full sample of 20 classrooms at each grade level.

In Sendai and Taipei, permission from educational authorities and school principals was sufficient to allow us to test the children. The procedure was less simple in Minneapolis, where interviews were held with school administrators of 15 independent school systems in order to arrange for the recruitment of subjects.

All children in the classrooms—a total of 4,260 children—were given a reading test. The remaining tests and interviews were given to target samples of 240 children and their mothers in each grade in each city. These target samples of children were constituted by randomly selecting two boys and two girls from the upper, middle, and lower thirds of the distribution of reading scores obtained in each classroom. In Minneapolis, parental permission had to be obtained before a child could participate in the study. Parents were very cooperative; only 38 of the 863 parents we contacted refused permission to test their children. The actual number of children ultimately included in the American, Chinese, and Japanese target samples at each grade ranged between 237 and 246.

The mean age of the first graders at the beginning of the study was 6.7 years in Taipei and 6.8 years in Sendai and Minneapolis. The respective standard deviations were .4, .4, and .3 years. Mean ages for the fifth graders were 10.8 years in Taipei and 10.9 years in Sendai and Minneapolis. The standard deviations were the same as those obtained for first graders. All but four children in the American sample were born in the United States; approximately 1% were from minority families. Thus, the American sample contained predominantly white, English-speaking, native-born, urban children.

Children who were mentally retarded or who had serious linguistic, emotional, or personal problems were identified by the teachers and were excluded from the study. Only 15 children from the 120 classrooms were excluded for these reasons.

PHASES OF THE STUDY

Each phase of the study occurred at the same point in the school year of each country. The initial phase was conducted in 1980–81 and the follow-up of the original first graders in 1984–85, when the children were in the fifth grade.

Interviews with the children's mothers took place after the children were tested. It was possible to arrange interviews with 87% of the American, 96% of the Chinese, and 99% of the Japanese parents in the target samples. Over 90% of the interviews were with mothers; of the remainder, 2% were with fathers and 2% with both parents.

In the follow-up study, efforts were made in Sendai and Taipei to include all children who still attended the schools in which they originally had been enrolled. This resulted in samples of 164 children in Taipei and 167 children in Sendai. Interviews were arranged with 110 mothers of the children in Taipei and of 159 in Sendai. In Minneapolis, efforts were made to contact parents directly, whether or not the child was still enrolled in the school that he or she had attended in the first grade. The follow-up sample in Minneapolis included 121 children and 120 mothers.

EXAMINERS

Examiners and interviewers were residents of the cities in which the study was conducted. They were either persons who had worked professionally with children or students enrolled in programs in social work or education. Examiners were carefully trained in testing and interviewing procedures by the coordinators of the project in each city. A total of approximately 100 men and women, ranging in age from their early twenties to their late thirties, served as examiners and interviewers. Assignment of individuals was determined by availability rather than by any systematic matching between examiners, interviewers, and subjects. Rarely did the same person interview the mother of a child that he or she had tested or interviewed.

MONOGRAPHS

ACHIEVEMENT TESTS

Comparative studies of children's scholastic achievement must use culturally fair, interesting, and psychometrically sound tests. To meet these goals, a team of bilingual researchers from each culture constructed achievement tests with the aim of eliminating cultural bias as much as possible. Carefully written instructions in all three languages and personal contact with the supervisors helped produce comparable testing procedures in the three cities. The content of the tests is described in detail in Stevenson et al. (1982) and Stigler, Lee, Lucker, and Stevenson (1982).

The reading test contained three types of items: sight-reading of vocabulary, reading of meaningful text material, and comprehension of text. The tests were based on detailed analyses of the vocabulary, grammar, and content of two of the most popular text series in the United States, the single series used in Taiwan, and two of the most popular Japanese series. This information made it possible for us to construct reading tests that were comparable across the three languages according to reading level.

Kindergarten items involved matching, naming, and identifying letters in English, *zhuyin fuhao* in Chinese, and *hiragana* in Japanese. The vocabulary portion of the test assessed children's ability to sight-read single isolated words. In grades 1–3, the words were common to all three languages, but, in grades 4–6, the small number of new vocabulary items common to the three languages made it necessary to use different words in the three forms of the test. Selection of these words was based on two factors: similar frequencies of usage and introduction for the first time at the particular grade. The part of the test involving reading and comprehending text contained items tapping the child's ability to read text presented in clauses, paragraphs, and sentences. Three types of items were included: phrases or sentences describing one of three pictures, sentences in which key words were omitted but for which three alternatives were provided, and paragraphs about which questions were asked. Intercorrelations among the three portions of the test ranged from .74 to .97 (N's = 410–932), indicating that the test is highly reliable.

Prior to constructing the mathematics tests, analyses were made of the time at which each mathematical concept and operation was introduced in the textbook series used in Sendai and Taipei and in the series used by the majority of schools in the Minneapolis metropolitan area. A master list included a total of 320 concepts and skills. Because the concepts were not always introduced at the same time in the three series, it was impossible to construct a useful test involving only concepts that appeared simultaneously in all three curricula. We sought, therefore, to sample what we believed were the most important elements. The final test included 70 questions. Of the concepts assessed, all but one appeared in the Japanese curriculum, all but four in the American curriculum, and all but six in the Chinese curriculum. Some items required only computation; others required application of mathematical principles to word problems. The test proved to be interesting and very reliable. Values of the Cronbach alpha, computed separately by grade and country, ranged from .92 to .96 (N's = 237–246).

All achievement tests were administered individually to each child. Tests were not timed, and the child continued to the point of failing over a quarter of the items in the reading test at a grade level and of failing four successive questions in the mathematics test. The tests were administered in the same manner during the first and follow-up phases of the study in Minneapolis and Sendai. In Taipei, the tests were administered comparably during the first phase but to small groups of children in the follow-up study.

The reading test was given approximately 4 months after the beginning of the school year, and the mathematics test was given 2 months later. The tests were given in one session in the follow-up study, but, because the time of testing differed somewhat in the three cities, cross-cultural comparisons of the results of the second testing are not appropriate. Interviews with the children were conducted in the original study during the session in which the mathematics test was given. In the follow-up study, tests and interviews were given in the single session.

INTERVIEWS AND QUESTIONNAIRES

Eighteen interviews and questionnaires were constructed for this study, six in each of the three languages. In the initial study, there were interviews for the mothers and children and questionnaires for the teachers and school principals. In the follow-up study, new interviews were constructed for the mothers and children. Because of their number and length, these materials are not reproduced in this *Monograph;* however, they are available on request from the authors.

MOTHER INTERVIEW

Great care was taken in constructing the interviews to ensure that the questions would be relevant in each culture and that their wording conveyed the same meaning in each language. Researchers from the United States, Taiwan, and Japan developed the interviews and coded the responses. All knew two of the languages and had studied the second one for many years; several had served as professional translators. We constructed the interviews simultaneously in all three languages, thereby avoiding the problems inevitably encountered when items are constructed in one language and then are translated into another one. In addition to these precautions, all items were reviewed by professionals in each culture. No system for constructing materials for cross-cultural studies is foolproof, but we believe that the procedures we followed resulted in interviews that corresponded very closely to each other in the three languages.

Some interview items required factual answers; in others, we sought the mothers' opinions. Mothers rated some of the items according to predefined scales; other items were open ended. Approximately half the questions were common to the interviews used for the two phases of the study. In the second interview with the mothers, emphasis was placed on the mothers' evaluations of factors that influence children's academic performance, their satisfaction with their child's performance, and their attributions about the bases of academic achievement. The interviews contained approximately 200 items.

Because of the great amount of work necessary for scoring open-ended questions, and because we were uncertain about whether mothers in the three cultures would be equally voluble, we included as many objective questions as possible. For these questions, the interviewer read the alternative responses to the mother and placed a card listing them in front of her.

All coding was done at the University of Michigan. Coding schemes and rating scales developed for the open-ended questions were made as explicit as possible and contained many examples. All interviews were coded twice by native speakers of the relevant language who worked independently of each other. The coding scheme was so explicit that it was not difficult for two coders to obtain over 90% agreement for coding the open-ended questions. In some cases, differences in coding were a result of simple errors that could be easily corrected. In the cases in which the two coders could not resolve a disagreement, a final rating was decided on after group discussion that included at least two representatives of each of the three cultures.

Mothers were interviewed at home, and the children were interviewed at school. We encountered no major problems in conducting the interviews. They required from 60 to 90 min to complete, and, despite many warnings we had received about the difficulties we would encounter in getting the mothers to respond freely to our questions, most mothers were judged to be appropriately responsive. Nearly all American and Chinese mothers and 80% of the Japanese mothers were judged by the interviewer to be responsive, and over 90% were considered to be friendly and cooperative. Nearly all the American and Japanese mothers seemed to understand what was being asked of them; however, perhaps because of their comparatively lower level of education, 18% of the Taipei mothers were judged to have a poor understanding of the questions. When mothers appeared not to understand a question, the interviewer repeated the question and attempted to clarify whatever had not been understood. Mothers had little difficulty in making ratings after the procedure had been explained.

TEACHER QUESTIONNAIRE

Information from teachers was obtained by a questionnaire they filled out at home; all 120 teachers of the classrooms we visited were willing to cooperate with us in this manner. The procedures used in constructing this questionnaire and coding the responses were the same as those used for the parent interview. About 70 questions contained in the interview covered teachers' educational background, beliefs about teaching, classroom management, and the teacher's daily schedule. Additional information about the schools was obtained from an interview with the principal of each school.

CHILD INTERVIEW

In the initial study, the children were asked to make a series of ratings to indicate their attitudes about homework, arithmetic, reading, and going to school. The rating procedure was demonstrated by asking them to indicate how much they liked to watch television by pointing to one of five faces with expressions ranging from a broad smile to a deep frown. The interview required only a few minutes.

The interview with children in the follow-up study contained an extensive set of questions. Typically, at least 20 min were required to answer all 78 questions included in the interview. They were focused on children's attitudes about school and their reasons for holding these attitudes, self-evaluations of characteristics such as level of achievement and intellectual ability, explanations of academic success and failure, and attitudes about mathematics and reading. All items were presented in the form of seven-point rating scales. If a child appeared to have difficulty reading the questions, the examiner read them aloud. All interviews were coded twice to eliminate errors.

III. ACHIEVEMENT IN READING AND MATHEMATICS

Interpreting the scores from the mathematics test was relatively straightforward because their distributions were represented satisfactorily by the means and standard deviations obtained at each grade in each city (see Fig. 1). Performance on the reading test is more difficult to describe; as is evident in Figure 2, the distributions of scores were highly skewed. A small number of first graders in each city were capable of reading at the highest level of the test, whereas some fifth graders were incapable of reading at more than the first- or second-grade level. Thus, in addition to analyses of variance of the levels of performance, analyses also are presented of the percentage of children performing at grade level and of the top and bottom scorers.

LEVELS OF PERFORMANCE

The average scores on the reading test appear in Table 1. Chinese children obtained the highest scores on all three parts of the test at grade 1 and on the vocabulary and comprehension sections at grade 5. Japanese children obtained the lowest scores.

The mathematics test contained items that involved application of mathematical principles to the solution of word problems and items requiring only calculation. American children did significantly more poorly than Chinese and Japanese children on both types of items at both grades (see Table 1). The Asian children's superiority in mathematics was not limited, therefore, to facility in mathematical computation; they also were more successful in using their knowledge about mathematics in solving problems. Scores for these two types of items were highly correlated at both the first (r's = .69–.74) and the fifth grades (r's = .75–.84), all p's < .001.

The relative status of children who were followed up was stable between

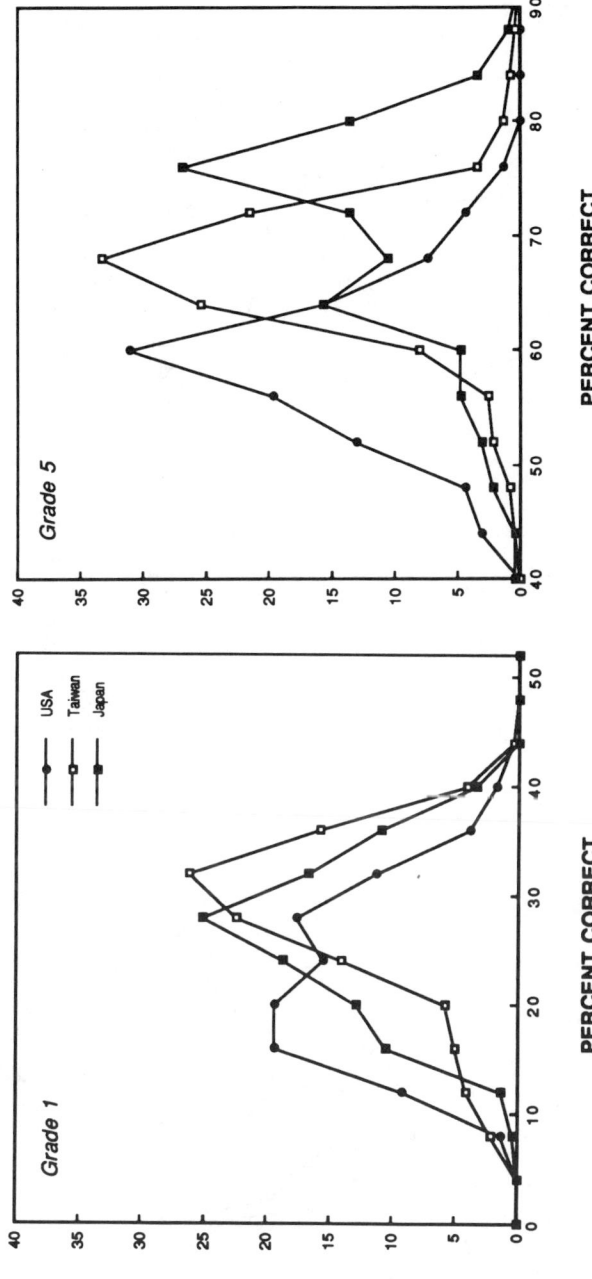

FIG. 1.—Frequency distributions of summary scores obtained for mathematics by first and fifth graders in each city.

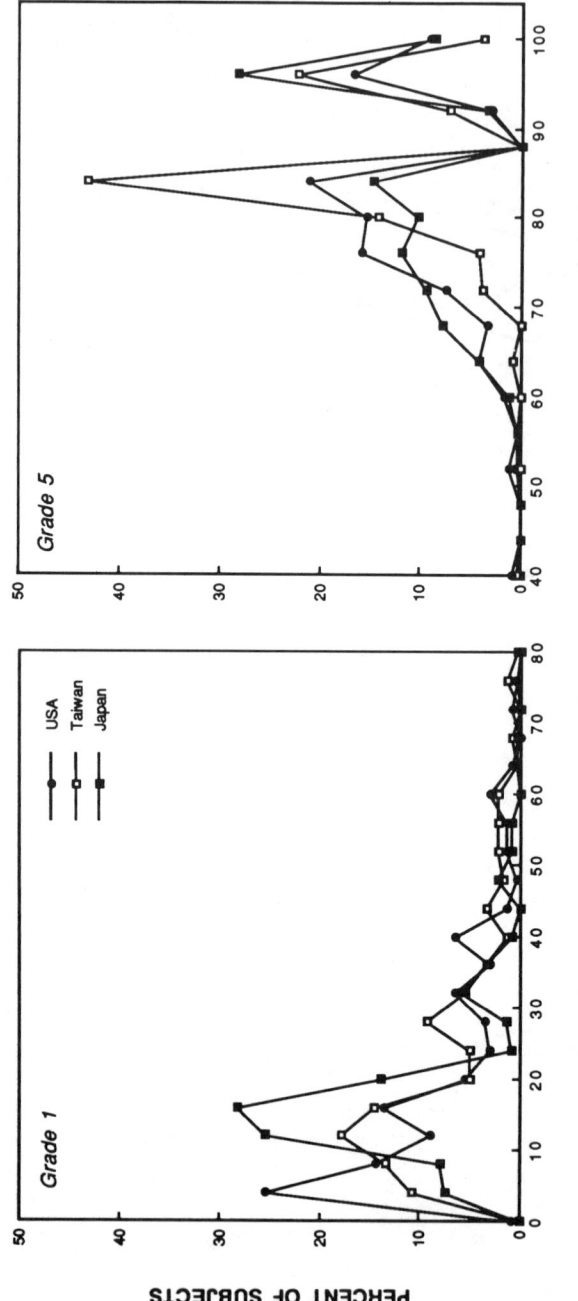

FIG. 2.—Frequency distributions of summary scores obtained for reading by first and fifth graders in each city.

TABLE 1

MEAN SCORES AND STANDARD DEVIATIONS OF READING AND MATHEMATICS TESTS

	READING				
	United States	Taiwan	Japan	F	Scheffé Contrasts
Grade 1:					
Vocabulary	9.95	10.78	7.16	12.09	T > J; U > J
	(9.63)	(9.11)	(6.21)	[.001]	[.001] [.001]
Comprehension . . .	21.27	25.65	22.76	4.16	T > U
	(18.23)	(18.68)	(13.17)	[.05]	[.05]
Reading text[a]	.17	.20	.15	4.19	T > J
	(.18)	(.21)	(.13)	[.01]	[.05]
Grade 5:					
Vocabulary	48.43	49.79	46.98	6.65	T > J
	(9.13)	(7.13)	(8.99)	[.01]	[.01]
Comprehension . . .	82.65	84.58	82.53	4.09	T > J
	(10.49)	(7.16)	(8.53)	[.05]	[.05]
Reading text[a]	.85	.85	.85	.17	. . .
	(.12)	(.11)	(.09)	[N.S.]	
	MATHEMATICS				
Grade 1:					
Operations	14.30	16.83	15.69	29.27	T > J > U
	(3.73)	(3.66)	(3.45)	[.001]	[.01] [.001]
Problem solving . . .	2.81	4.34	4.38	43.53	T & J > U
	(2.03)	(2.18)	(2.08)	[.001]	[.001]
Grade 5:					
Operations	32.27	36.17	37.15	72.84	T & J > U
	(4.98)	(3.21)	(5.65)	[.001]	[.001]
Problem solving . . .	11.71	14.59	15.68	107.00	J > T > U
	(2.69)	(2.91)	(3.62)	[.001]	[.001] [.001]

NOTE.—Standard deviations are given in parentheses and p levels in brackets. df's = 2,715 (grade 1), 2,725 (grade 5). All between-country comparisons are based on Scheffé contrasts: U = United States; T = Taiwan; J = Japan.
[a] Percentage correct.

the first and the second administrations of the mathematics and reading tests in all three cities. All three correlations between first- and fifth-grade vocabulary scores were .56; correlations for the comprehension scores were .50 (Minneapolis), .53 (Taipei), and .41 (Sendai). The correlations between first- and fifth-grade mathematics scores were high: .62, .57, and .63 for the American, Chinese, and Japanese children, respectively. All these correlations are highly significant, p's < .001.

Scores in reading and mathematics were also positively related to each other in the first and fifth grades in the initial study and in the fifth grade in the follow-up study. The correlations ranged from .51 to .60 in Minneapolis, from .44 to .56 in Taipei, and from .52 to .64 in Sendai, all p's < .001.

MONOGRAPHS

SUMMARY SCORES

To simplify analyses involving the achievement scores, summary scores were created. For reading, the summary score was represented by the average percentage of correct responses on all three portions of the reading test. In the follow-up study, it included only the vocabulary and reading comprehension subtests because the procedure used to evaluate the performance of reading of text differed slightly in Taipei and in the other two cities. For mathematics, summary scores represented the percentage of total items correct. An overall summary score, used in exploring the relation of achievement with familial and experiential variables, was obtained by averaging the summary scores for reading and mathematics.

ADVANCED VERSUS SLOW READERS

Another way of comparing the performance of children in the three cultures is to determine the percentage of children whose level of skill was appropriate for their grade in school. In the reading test, children were allowed to go to items at the next grade level if they could answer more than 75% of the comprehension and vocabulary items at their own grade level. The proportion of first graders who were able to do so was 60% in Minneapolis, 78% in Taipei, and 86% in Sendai, $\chi^2(2, N = 718) = 45.85, p < .001$. The performance of the Chinese and Japanese children is especially notable because, being tested four months after beginning school, the test included some characters whose meaning and pronunciation would not be taught until later in the school year. Thus, fewer American than Chinese or Japanese first graders were able to advance beyond the first grade level of the reading test.

The percentage of fifth graders who were unable to meet the criteria for reading at the fourth-grade level and who might be considered to be poor readers was 31% in Minneapolis but only 12% in Taipei and 21% in Sendai, $\chi^2(2, N = 728) = 28.21, p < .001$. Under the most extreme criterion of being more than 2 years behind in reading level—a common definition of reading disability—the respective percentages dropped to 3%, 2%, and 8%. We conclude that there were more poor readers among the American fifth graders but not more children with severe reading problems.

These data may appear to be at odds with those describing the average levels of performance. In fact, the latter do not differ because the percentage of fifth graders reading above grade level was also higher in Minneapolis (40%) than in Taipei (33%) or Sendai (29%), $\chi^2(2, N = 728) = 7.00, p < .05$.

The explanation of why so many American fifth graders were both below and above their grade level in reading may be related, in part, to the possibility of breaking down English words by sound. This characteristic of alphabetic writing systems is not shared by written Chinese or Japanese, where the pronunciation and meaning of characters must be taught and memorized. Individual differences in reading have often been explained by differences in the ability of American children to segment words into their component phonemes (e.g., Stanovich, 1987). Children who are not skilled in doing so have difficulty in reading, whereas those who understand how this is done can decode words they have never seen before. Another possible explanation may lie in the practices for handling slow and fast learners. Children in American classrooms are divided into reading groups, with fast learners reading more advanced materials and slower learners reading easier ones. This never occurs in Chinese or Japanese classrooms. Regardless of how well or how poorly they read, all children must adhere to the rate of progress prescribed in the national curriculum. It is unlikely that Chinese or Japanese children will learn characters at school that are more advanced than those contained in the reading curriculum for their grade. Learning characters beyond a child's grade level must occur outside the classroom.

TOP AND BOTTOM SCORERS

In a third type of comparison, we determined the number of children from each city who received the highest and the lowest scores from all three cities combined. Scores for all children in the subsample were combined into a single distribution at each grade for reading and for mathematics, and the number of children from each city included in the top and bottom 100 scores was determined.

If children from the three cities performed equally well, approximately 33 children from each city should be among the top and bottom scorers on the reading tests. American children were overrepresented in the bottom 100 scores in both grades. For example, among the 100 children with the lowest scores on the vocabulary and reading comprehension portions of the test, there were, respectively, 47 and 56 American first graders and 44 and 47 American fifth graders. However, as can be seen in Figure 3, American children were also well represented among those receiving top scores. Thus, it is difficult to characterize the reading skill of the American children compared to the Chinese and Japanese children. A sizable group of the American children were reading beyond their grade level, but there was also a disproportionate number of American children who were poor readers.

The distribution of the top and bottom 100 scores in mathematics according to country provides a dramatic illustration of the American children's poor performance (see Fig. 3). Of those receiving the 100 lowest

MONOGRAPHS

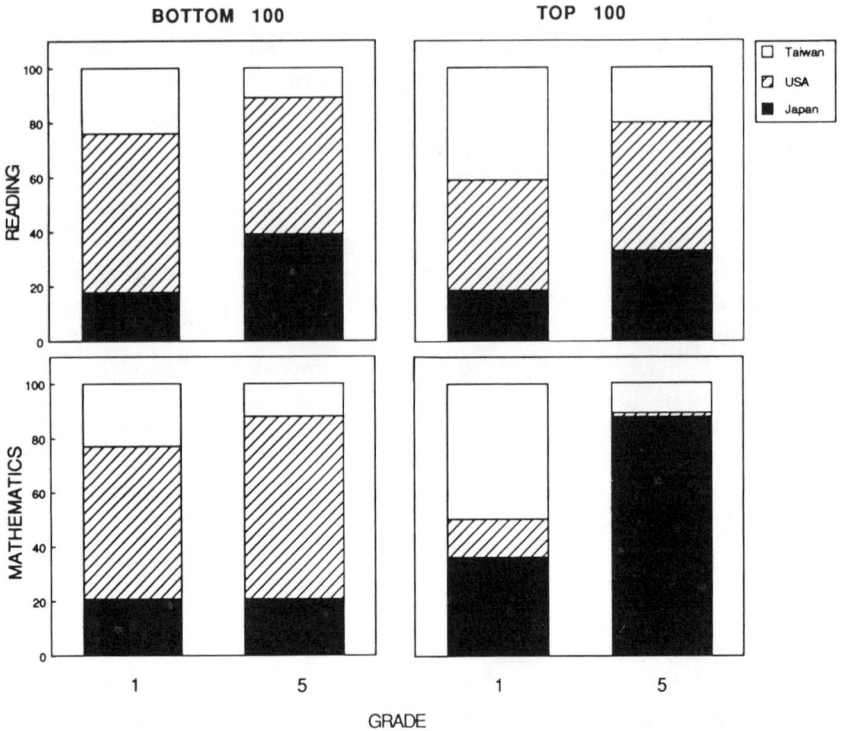

FIG. 3.—Distribution of the top 100 and bottom 100 scorers in distributions of summary scores for reading and mathematics tests according to location.

scores at the first grade, 56 were American children, and, of those receiving the 100 lowest scores at the fifth grade, 67 were American children. Only 14 American children were among those receiving the top 100 scores at the first grade. Only one American child was among those receiving the top 100 scores at the fifth grade.

VARIABILITY

The design of the study made it possible to partition the total variance in achievement scores obtained within each location into that due to individual differences within each classroom, differences between classrooms within each school, and differences among schools. We used the summary scores for reading and mathematics achievement for examining these effects.

Variability among individuals within each classroom provides an index of the diversity of students encountered by the teachers. The between-classroom variability reflects differences in the achievement levels of children attending different classrooms within each school. The between-school variability makes it possible to compare the degree of heterogeneity of achievement among different schools in the three cities.

Total variances in achievement scores were partitioned into these three components.[1] The results are depicted in Figure 4. It is obvious that in all three cities the preponderant source of variability was among individuals within each classroom. Variability existed among schools, but there was no evidence of a significant portion of variability being attributable to variability between classrooms within schools.

If the goal of education is to reduce individual differences among children—as is sometimes stated by Japanese educators—scores should be less variable among fifth graders than among first graders. Partial support for this goal was found for the reading scores. Variability in reading scores decreased between the first and the fifth grades in Minneapolis and Taipei and remained the same in Sendai. In mathematics, variability tended to increase between the first and the fifth grades. The differences were significant in Sendai and in Minneapolis.

Variability among individuals within classrooms.—The analyses of the Minneapolis data gave little support to arguments sometimes made that teaching in American elementary schools is especially difficult because of the great diversity in children's levels of achievement within each classroom. In this instance, at least, the argument does not hold. In all three cities, almost all the variance among children's performance in both reading and mathematics can be attributed to variability among individuals within the classrooms.

Variability among schools.—Variability among schools in reading scores differed significantly among the three cities at both the first and the fifth grades. Reading scores were most variable among the schools in Minneapolis. Variability in mathematics scores differed significantly among the schools at the first grade, with the greatest variability among the schools of Taipei. By the fifth grade, differences among schools in mathematics scores

---

[1] The procedures for calculating the total variance of achievement at individual, classroom, and school levels are as follows: the individual variances within classroom = MS (mean square) individual, which is the MS error for one-way analysis of variance using classroom as predictor. The between-classroom variance within school = (MS class − MS individual)/N of children per class. The between-school variance = (MS school − MS class)/N of children per school. MS school is derived from the MS between from one-way analysis of variance using school as predictor. And MS class = (SS [sum of squares] class − SS school)/(total N of classes − total N of schools). The procedures were done separately for each country, for each grade, and for reading and mathematics achievement. We are grateful to David A. Kenny for his suggestion of this procedure.

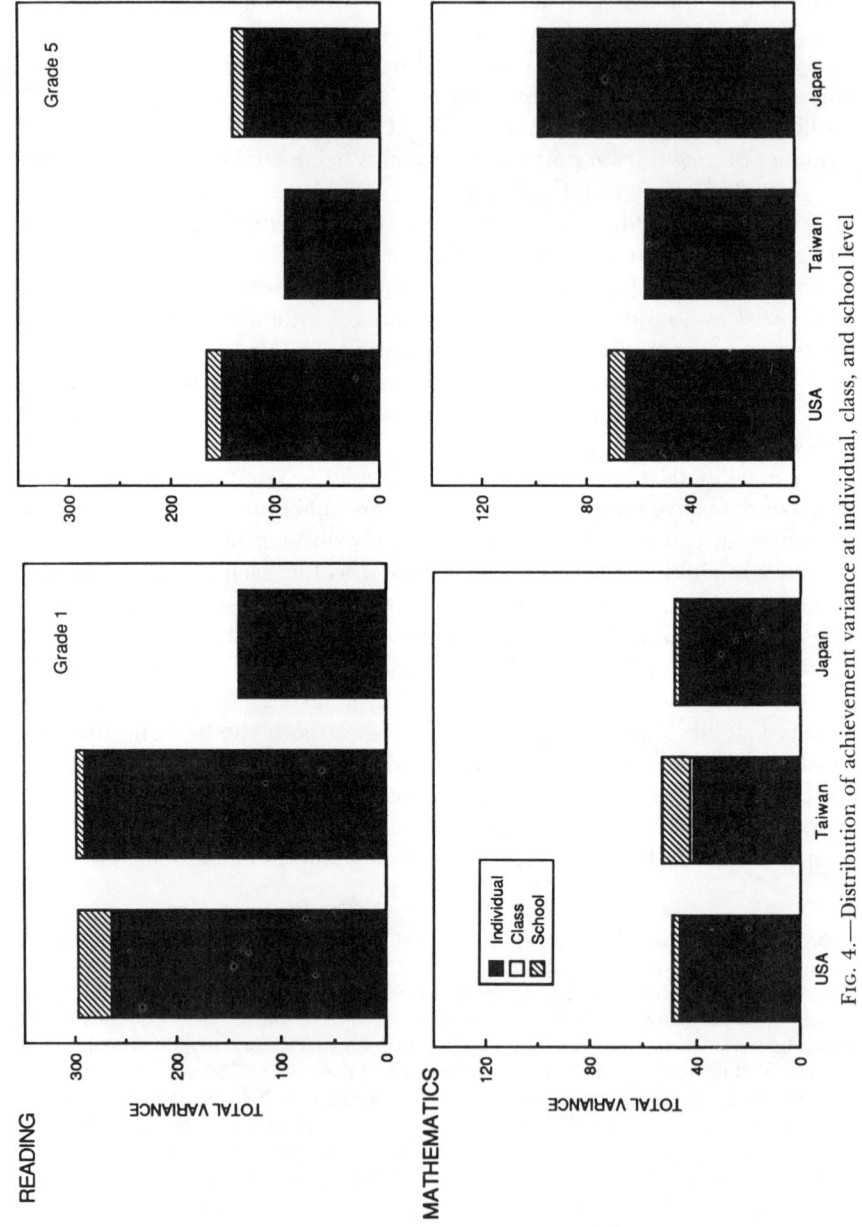

FIG. 4.—Distribution of achievement variance at individual, class, and school level

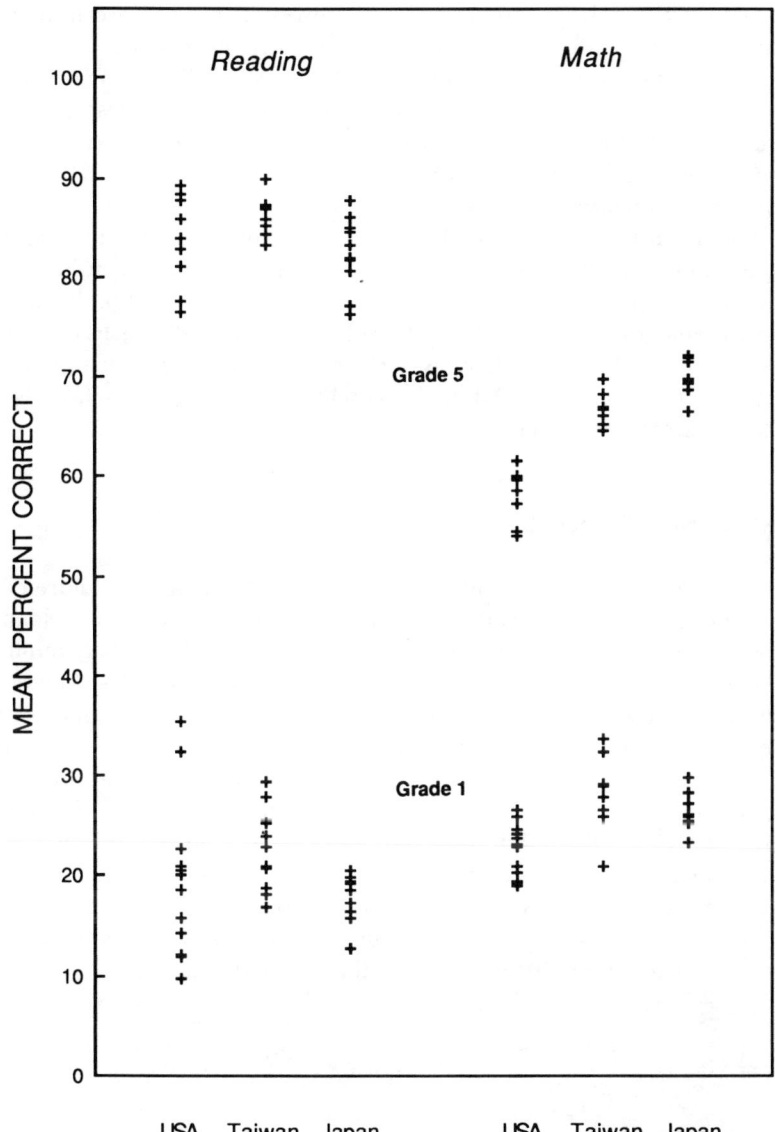

FIG. 5.—Mean percentage of correct responses in each school at the first and fifth grades in reading and mathematics.

were significant only in Minneapolis. These results are of special interest because children in Taipei and Sendai attend schools that follow a clearly prescribed national curriculum, whereas those in Minneapolis do not. Moreover, neighborhoods in different parts of Japanese and Chinese cities are more similar to each other than are those in large American cities. Both these factors may account for the tendency for variance to be greatest among the Minneapolis schools.

The mean reading and mathematics scores for each school are represented graphically in terms of percentage of correct responses in Figure 5. There was a high degree of overlap among the distributions of both reading and mathematics scores for the first grade among the schools in the three cities. At the fifth grade, there is a clear separation in the mathematics scores; the highest-scoring Minneapolis school was below the schools with the lowest scores in Sendai and Taipei.

CONCLUDING COMMENTS

Compared to the Taipei and Sendai children, Minneapolis children did poorly in mathematics during the elementary school years. The evidence concerning reading was more ambiguous; while a disproportionate number of American children could be classified as poor readers, some American children also did well in reading. These results cannot be explained by differences in the children's exposure to the materials used in the tests, for both the reading and the mathematics tests were based on the textbooks used by the children in each city. Nor can they be explained by the conditions under which the children were tested. All tests, except in the Taipei follow-up study, were given individually to the children by trained examiners from their own cities. The underlying causes are much more complex. The major goal of the remaining discussion is to describe conditions that may account for these differences in children's performance.

IV. BACKGROUND INFORMATION: SCHOOLS AND TEACHERS

Background information about the structure and operation of schools is helpful in understanding children's achievement, especially when comparisons are made between schools that differ as markedly as those in Taipei, Sendai, and Minneapolis. The interviews with the teachers and principals of the schools revealed some of the important characteristics of each school system; these, as well as daily classroom practices, are described in this section.

SCHOOLS

Enrollment in the 13 Minneapolis schools that participated in the study ranged from 250 to 800 pupils, with an average of 500 students. Most schools were in quiet residential areas scattered throughout the large metropolitan area; few schools were located in busy parts of the city. There were 410 first graders and 453 fifth graders in the 40 Minneapolis classrooms, resulting in an average class size of 21 at the first grade and 23 at the fifth grade.

Taipei schools are large and crowded. Like the city itself, they must accommodate a population that has outgrown available physical facilities. Many schools are located in busy sections of the city where there is heavy traffic of vehicles and people. The number of children attending the elementary schools we visited averaged 2,790, with the populations ranging from 1,970 to 4,460, except for one school with 390 pupils. There was an average of 10 classrooms at each grade level, each enrolling 45 students at the first grade and 48 at the fifth grade. The classrooms included in our study contained 912 first graders and 956 fifth graders.

Sendai schools were intermediate in size. Each typically had from three to five classrooms, with an average of 39 children in both first- and fifth-grade classrooms. The average population of the schools was 1,020 children and ranged from 740 to 1,260. Like the Minneapolis schools, most of the schools in Sendai occupied relatively large plots of land in residential areas of the city. The classrooms included in the study contained 785 first and 744 fifth graders.

Despite the large classes, teachers in Taipei and Sendai are able to know their pupils well. In contrast to Minneapolis, where teachers often remain with the same children for only one year, teachers in Japan and Taiwan usually remain with one group of children for 2 years and in Sendai sometimes for 3 years. The populations of the schools were stable; the principals estimated that 75% of the children in the Minneapolis metropolitan area, 88% in Taipei, and 68% in Sendai remain in the same school throughout all 6 years of elementary school.

Chinese and Japanese teachers' acquaintance with their pupils is enhanced by visits to the children's homes, once a year in Sendai and twice a year in Taipei. Home visits were made by teachers in only three of the Minneapolis schools. Communication between parents and teachers in Japan and Taiwan is also carried on with the aid of little notebooks (*lianluobu* in Chinese and *renrakucho* in Japanese) that children carry back and forth to school. The mother must check in the notebook that the child has completed the daily homework assignment and may write about any general problems or difficulties of which the teacher should be aware. In turn, the notebooks are used by teachers to communicate with parents about homework assignments, test results, special activities in school, and the child's behavior. Parents and teachers are expected to check the notebook every day. No such established way of communicating with parents exists for American teachers.

Open houses are held at the schools in each city at least once a year. According to the school principals, they are attended on the average by 65% of the mothers and 25% of the fathers in Minneapolis; the parallel values are 45% and 10% in Taipei and 80% and 5% in Sendai. Thus, despite their intense interest in their children's education, the percentage of Asian parents who use the opportunity to visit their child's classroom does not greatly exceed that of American parents.

The school year is longer in Taipei and Sendai than in Minneapolis, averaging 174 days a year in Minneapolis, 230 in Taipei, and 243 in Sendai. In Minneapolis, children attend school Monday through Friday; in Taipei and Sendai, they also attend school for a half day on Saturday. Daily attendance at school was high in all three cities; we estimate a rate of absence of 2.7% in Minneapolis, 3.8% in Sendai, and a remarkably low .1% in Taipei (Stevenson et al., 1987).

For first graders, the school day is longer in Minneapolis (6 hours) than in Taipei (4 hours) or Sendai (5 hours). The same schedule is followed at the fifth grade in Minneapolis, but Taipei fifth graders are in school each weekday for 8.3 hours (except for one 6-hour day). Fifth graders in Sendai attend school an average of 6.5 hours each weekday. There is great similarity in the schedules for different classrooms in Taipei and Sendai; in Minneapolis, schedules differ greatly, not only among schools, but also among classrooms within a school.

The daily session of elementary schools in the Minneapolis metropolitan area began shortly after 9:00 A.M. and ended between 2:30 and 3:00 P.M. In Japan and Taiwan, it began between 8:00 and 8:30 A.M., and children could remain at school until after 4:00 P.M. to participate in various clubs and activities after formal classes ended.

The school day was highly structured in Taipei and Sendai, with 40–45 minutes of class followed by a 10–15 minute break. Western visitors frequently comment about the rapt attention and intense concentration of children in Chinese and Japanese classrooms. This ability to focus so closely on academic activities may be due in part to the opportunity for vigorous play provided by the between-class breaks. Minneapolis schools had no more than two recesses a day. This is in striking contrast with the average of four recesses at the first grade in Sendai and Taipei and of eight at the fifth grade in Taipei and five in Sendai. Demands for protracted concentration without frequent opportunities for play may contribute to the wandering attention that was observed among these children (e.g., Stevenson et al., 1987). Japanese and Chinese teachers found it unbelievable that the children in Minneapolis had only one or two recesses a day and that school buildings were empty shortly after the last class period ended.

From all these data, we can estimate the total number of hours spent in school during the school year. First graders in all three educational systems spent from 1,044 to 1,162 hours in school. In the fifth grade, however, children attended school for 1,044 hours a year in Minneapolis, for 1,655 hours in Taipei, and for 1,466 hours in Sendai. (These estimates included lunch hours and after-class activities.) These schedules remained the same between grades 2 and 6; thus, the fifth-grade estimates apply to these grades as well. We believe that the extra opportunities for instruction and practice available to Chinese and Japanese children must play an important role in their academic achievement.

CURRICULUM

The general rule in Chinese and Japanese schools is that children remain with their classmates and follow the same curriculum throughout elementary school, regardless of the students' academic progress. In Minneapolis, as in many American schools, slow learners were assigned to special classrooms, or children in the same class were divided into different reading or mathematics levels, each pursuing somewhat different curricula. All children in Sendai and Taipei classrooms are promoted each year. The Minneapolis schools also generally promote all children to the next grade, although from 1% to 6% of the children were required to repeat the grade in some schools.

The high degree of local autonomy found in American school systems does not exist in Asian countries. In Taiwan, educational policy is highly centralized, with a curriculum specified by the Ministry of Education for all schools, including private ones. Textbooks and teachers' manuals are published by the Ministry of Education, and every school uses the same set of textbooks. These practices do not occur in public schools in the United States, where local school boards, principals, and at times even individual teachers make their own choices about the curriculum and textbooks. In Japan, a national curriculum is defined by the Ministry of Education, which also publishes detailed descriptions of what is to be accomplished at each grade and in what order. Private publishers of textbooks follow this curriculum, thereby making several series of textbooks for each subject available to Japanese schools.

Estimates of the amount of time spent on reading and mathematics in the classrooms of the three cities can be made from the observational data we collected in each classroom (Stevenson et al., 1987). These were based on 1,200 observational periods in Sendai, 1,353 in Minneapolis, and 1,600 in Taipei. Each observational period lasted approximately 40 min and took place over 2 weeks according to a randomly generated schedule covering the hours children were in school. We estimate that the American children spent approximately 3 hours a week in mathematics; the Chinese and Japanese children, especially at the fifth grade, were estimated to spend over twice that amount of time (see Table 2).[2] In terms of the percentage of

---

[2] It should be noted that these data are in line with but not identical to those described in the official curricula of Taiwan and Japan or in the reports of Minneapolis principals. For example, the amount of time devoted to language arts vs. mathematics in the official fifth-grade curriculum for Taiwan schools is 6.8 vs. 3.9 hours and in the official Japanese curriculum 4.5 vs. 3.8 hours. Because there is no standard curriculum in American schools, we relied on principals' reports. The Minneapolis principals estimated that fifth graders spent an average of 11.4 hours a week on reading and 4.4 hours a week on mathematics. The ratios of these values were 2.6:1 in Minneapolis, 1.7:1 in Taipei, and 1.2:1 in Sendai. The ratios of the time spent on reading vs. mathematics derived from our observations were, correspondingly, 2.3:1, .9:1, and 1.0:1. The discrepancies in Taipei and Sendai may be due, in part, to the fact that our observations were conducted in both the morning and the afternoon, but mathematics is typically taught only in the morning in these schools.

TABLE 2

Estimates of the Number of Hours Spent Each Week in
Language Arts (Reading) and Mathematics

	United States	Taiwan	Japan
Grade 1:			
Language arts	10.5	10.4	8.7
Mathematics	2.7	4.0	5.8
Grade 5:			
Language arts	7.9	11.1	8.0
Mathematics	3.4	11.7	7.8

instructional time devoted to these subjects, the American fifth graders, for example, spent more than 40% of classroom time on language arts, whereas children in the other two cities spent less than 30% of classroom time on this subject. At neither grade did the American children spend as much as 20% of their classroom time studying mathematics. This was lower than the percentage for either the Chinese or the Japanese children. At the fifth grade, reading and mathematics occupied approximately equal percentages of time for the Chinese and Japanese children, but the American children spent more than twice as much time on reading as on mathematics. It seems likely to us that the poor performance of the American children in mathematics may be traced, in part, to this large difference in the time they were engaged in activities related to mathematics.

TEACHERS

Background.—The Minneapolis teachers had many more years of formal education than did teachers in Taiwan and Japan; all 40 were college graduates, and 11 had advanced degrees. Most of the Chinese teachers (35 out of 40) were graduates of a 5-year teacher training program that they entered after completing middle school; one had a bachelor's degree. Of the 40 Japanese teachers, 27 had a bachelor's degree, typically in elementary education, but none had graduate training. The remaining teachers in Taiwan and Japan attended other types of colleges or, in a few cases in Taiwan, only high school.

The teachers were experienced professionals, with an average of 15 years of teaching experience among the Minneapolis group and an average of 17 years in both Taipei and Sendai. Most of the American and Chinese teachers were women; there were only four men in Minneapolis and eight in Taipei. Among the 40 teachers in Sendai, however, 18 were men.

In all but three Minneapolis schools, there were special teachers in music, physical education, remedial reading, and learning disabilities. Special teachers for the latter two areas do not exist in Taipei and Sendai schools, but there were special teachers for music, art, physical education, and home economics. The absence of special teachers for children with learning problems, emotional disturbance, or mild forms of mental retardation, coupled with the lack of school psychologists or social workers, means that the task of handling problem children or children with various forms of disability in Taipei and Sendai schools devolves on the regular teachers.

Professional life.—The teachers liked their work. The mean rating of degree of satisfaction with being a teacher was 7.7 for the American teachers, 6.3 for the Chinese teachers, and 6.8 for the Japanese teachers on a scale on which 1 was "very dissatisfied" and 9 was "very satisfied." Factors that maintained the teachers' interest in a teaching career were similar in the three cities. The most important factor was their interaction with children; this received mean ratings of 8.1, 8.3, and 7.9 by American, Chinese, and Japanese teachers on a scale with 9 defined as "very important." Despite the fact that teaching is held in high esteem in the Chinese and Japanese cultures, the teachers considered the prestige awarded to them by the community to be the least important of the eight factors they were asked to rate; the mean ratings made by American, Chinese, and Japanese teachers were 4.1, 4.8, and 3.7. Mean ratings for the remaining six factors were also similar across the three cities and, with few exceptions, were in the following order: personal development, contributing to society, interacting with colleagues, working schedule, physical conditions for work, and salary and fringe benefits.

Professional activities.—The Japanese teachers estimated that they spent an average of 51 hours at school each week, the Chinese teachers 47 hours, and the American teachers 42 hours. Teaching occupied an average of 28 hours each week for American and Japanese teachers; Chinese teachers spent an average of 30 hours. Since this time was spread out over 5½ days for the Chinese and Japanese teachers and over 5 days for the Americans, this meant that a greater percentage of each day's time was devoted to teaching by the American teachers.

Chinese and Japanese students were assigned greater responsibility for the management of the classrooms than was the case in the American schools; they exercised this responsibility through student government and classroom organizations. All but one of the schools in Taipei and all schools in Sendai had an organized student government; this was true for only three of the 13 Minneapolis schools. All schools in Sendai, six schools in Taipei, but only four schools in Minneapolis had classroom organizations. Furthermore, most janitorial duties in the Chinese and Japanese schools are assumed by the children.

CLASSROOM ACTIVITIES

Not only did the American children spend fewer days in school each year and fewer hours in school each day, but they also spent a lower percentage of school time participating in academic activities and a higher percentage engaged in other types of activities. First graders were observed to be engaged in academic activities 70%, 85%, and 79% of the time in Minneapolis, Taipei, and Sendai, respectively; the corresponding figures in fifth-grade classrooms were 64%, 92%, and 87%. Not only are the percentages lowest in the American classrooms at both grades, but fifth graders actually spent a lower percentage of their time on academic activities than did first graders.

Whereas Chinese and Japanese children were attending to the teacher over 60% of the time at both the first and the fifth grades, this occurred less than 50% of the time in the American classrooms, where children spent more time out of their seats, engaged in conversation with a peer and in other inappropriate activities. This was due, in part, to the manner in which the classrooms were organized. Minneapolis children were engaged in seatwork 44% of the time, Taipei children 34%, and Sendai children 33%. Typically, the Chinese and Japanese teachers remained in charge of the classroom when seatwork was conducted, but American teachers were more likely to spend the time in other activities, such as preparing lessons or grading papers. Such differences in classroom activities seem to us to exert an important influence on children's academic achievement. Further details on classroom activities are reported in Stevenson et al. (1987) and Stigler et al. (1987).

CONCLUDING COMMENTS

In our view, the large amounts of time spent in academic activities contributed to the superiority in academic achievement shown by the Chinese and Japanese children we studied. Indeed, the poor performance of our American sample becomes somewhat more understandable when one considers the shorter hours of the American school day and the school year and the briefer amounts of time spent on academic activities. Similarly, the great stress on reading and language arts in the Minneapolis elementary school curricula and the relative neglect of mathematics help clarify why performance among the American children in mathematics was so poor. Teachers appear to work hard in all three cities, but different obstacles are faced, depending on the size of the class, the presence of a national curriculum, the hours they must be responsible for their class, and the possibility of assistance from specialists.

V. BACKGROUND INFORMATION: FAMILIES AND CHILDREN

DEMOGRAPHIC CHARACTERISTICS

Parental education.—As can be seen in Table 3, the Minneapolis parents spent more years in school than the parents in the other two cities. Only 3% of the Minneapolis parents but 52% of the Chinese and 17% of the Japanese parents had less than a high school education. Differences were especially large for mothers; those in Taipei typically were graduates of middle school, but most Minneapolis and Sendai mothers had completed high school. Correlations between the average of the mothers' and fathers' level of education and their children's reading and mathematics scores ranged between .22 and .34, p's < .001; thus, approximately 10% of the variability in children's achievement scores could be accounted for by variability in parental education.

Father's occupation.—Because characteristics defining occupational status in one culture are not necessarily the same across cultures, the definition of the five occupational levels included in our scale—ranging from laborer to professional—had to be adjusted for each culture. For example, factors such as social prestige, level of education, size of the company, skill, and cleanliness of the workplace play a more important role in defining occupational level in Japan than they do in the United States. As can be seen in Table 4, the most frequent classification of fathers in Taipei and Sendai was skilled worker; in Minneapolis it was semiprofessional. The correlation between occupational status and level of education of fathers was .66 in Minneapolis, .70 in Taipei, and .86 in Sendai.

Family status.—The families were remarkably stable. Most children lived in intact families: 81% in Minneapolis, 97% in Taipei, and 95% in Sendai. Most of the families had resided in the same city during the child's whole life: 71%, 77%, and 64%, respectively. Families were smallest in Japan and largest in Taiwan: an average of 3.2 children in the Chinese, 2.9 in the American, and 2.3 in the Japanese families. Children in first- and later-born

TABLE 3

AVERAGE NUMBER OF YEARS OF EDUCATION OF MOTHERS AND FATHERS

	United States	Taiwan	Japan	F	Scheffé Contrasts
Mothers	13.6	8.7	12.0	330.75	U > J > T
	(2.1)	(4.2)	(1.9)	[.001]	[.001] [.001]
Fathers	14.7	10.9	13.0	126.78	U > J > T
	(3.1)	(4.4)	(2.7)	[.001]	[.001] [.001]

NOTE.—Standard deviations are given in parentheses and p levels in brackets. df's = 2,1342 (mothers); 2,1323 (fathers).

positions were equally represented in the three samples; the mean birth orders were 2.2, 2.3, and 1.7 in Minneapolis, Taipei, and Sendai.

Maternal employment.—Sixty-nine percent of the mothers in Minneapolis and 48% of the mothers in both Taipei and Sendai were employed. Considering full-time employment only, the percentage drops to 35% (Minneapolis), 33% (Taipei), and 30% (Sendai). Among mothers who were employed, only a few (8%) worked at home in Minneapolis, as compared to 28% in Taipei and 27% in Sendai.

The mothers' employment and educational status were unrelated, except in Japan, where the employed mothers had fewer years of education than the others (11.7 vs. 12.2 years). Mothers' employment status was not related to children's achievement at either the first or the fifth grade; average scores of children of employed and nonemployed mothers never differed by more than 1 point.

MATERNAL TEACHING BEFORE CHILD'S ENTRY TO SCHOOL

When mothers of first graders were asked whether they read regularly to their child, 76% of the American mothers but only 18% of the Chinese mothers and 50% of the Japanese mothers reported reading to their child

TABLE 4

PERCENTAGE OF FATHERS IN EACH OCCUPATIONAL LEVEL

	United States	Taiwan	Japan
Professional	18	5	3
Semiprofessional	43	20	26
Skilled	20	39	48
Semiskilled	11	30	20
Labor	1	4	0

either daily or several times each week. More American (66%) than Chinese (49%) or Japanese mothers (55%) of first graders also reported teaching their child the alphabet (*zhuyin fuhao, hiragana*) before entry to the first grade, $\chi^2(2, N = 677) = 13.76, p < .01$. The percentage who taught their children words (characters) was similar in the three cities (44%–47%), but more mothers in Taipei (36%) reported teaching their children to read whole sentences than in Sendai (29%) or Minneapolis (21%), $\chi^2(2, N = 676) = 12.25, p < .01$. This may be because combining characters to form sentences in Chinese is no more complicated than combining characters to form words—something that has no parallel in English or Japanese.

CHILDREN'S READING SKILLS BEFORE THE FIRST GRADE

We asked mothers and teachers of first graders whether the children could read letters, words, sentences, stories, and numbers when they entered school. (It seemed unlikely that mothers of the fifth graders could remember this information accurately.) Of the Sendai mothers, 78% reported that their child could read all the *hiragana* before entering the first grade; teachers in Sendai estimated that 73% of the first graders could do so. The estimates of Taipei mothers and teachers concerning the children who could read all the *zhuyin fuhao* were lower but very similar: 49% versus 43%. The American mothers and teachers showed far less agreement; 87% of the mothers reported that their children could read all the alphabet before entering the first grade, but the teachers estimated that only 50% of the children could do so.

Children's ability to read and understand words, sentences, and/or stories before the first grade differed greatly among the three cities. Among Japanese mothers, 57% reported that their children could read stories while still in kindergarten. In contrast, fewer than 20% of the Chinese and American mothers believed that their child could read stories. Teachers' estimates generally agreed with those of the mothers: 48% for the Japanese, 28% for the Chinese, and 12% for the American children. The advantage of a written syllabary with constant symbol-sound correspondence is immediately evident: a child who knows *hiragana* can easily read a story when it is written solely in *hiragana*. This is not the case with English letters; regardless of how well they know the alphabet, children still must be taught to read words. The same is true for Chinese; children find it nearly impossible to deduce the meaning or pronunciation of a Chinese character until these have been explained.

The American children were less likely than the Japanese or Chinese children to be able to write their names before they entered school. Again, there was less agreement between the opinions of mothers and teachers in

Minneapolis than in Sendai or Taipei. The American mothers estimated that 86% of the children could write their own names before entering school—a much larger percentage than the 61% reported by the teachers. Taipei and Sendai mothers' estimates were 94% and 100%, respectively—values that were in close accord with those made by the teachers in these two cities (99% and 100%).

A single score was created by summing the number of items dealing with preschool knowledge to which the mother responded positively. These included the children's ability to read the alphabet, words, sentences, stories, and numerals less than 10 and more than 10 and write their whole name. The mean score for Taipei children (T) was 4.2, for Minneapolis children (U) 6.2, and for Sendai children (J) 6.7, $F(2,678) = 152.79, p < .001$; U and J > T, p's < .001, J > U, $p < .05$. The correlations between these scores and first graders' scores on the reading test were .48, .35, and .37, respectively, for Minneapolis, Taipei, and Sendai. When preschool knowledge and mothers' level of education were both entered into regression equations predicting later achievement in reading, the preschool knowledge variable made a significant, unique contribution to the prediction of first-grade reading scores in all three locations (beta weights ranged from .30 to .42; overall $R^2 = .13-.26$).

The importance of preschool knowledge in predicting later achievement was given further emphasis in the follow-up study. In both Minneapolis and Sendai, these maternal estimates contributed significantly to the prediction of fifth-grade reading scores, even after the effects of maternal education and first-grade reading scores had been partialed out. (The beta weight for the preschool knowledge variable was .22 in Minneapolis and .20 in Sendai; overall $R^2 = .41$ and .34.) Overall prediction of fifth-grade reading scores was equally effective in Taipei ($R^2 = .41$), but inclusion of the preschool knowledge variable was not a significant factor in the regression equation (beta weight was .04).

PRESCHOOL EXPERIENCE

What children learn before entering the first grade may depend, in part, on the number of years they have spent in preschool. Three-, 4-, and 5-year-olds attend *yochien* in Japan and *youzhiyuan* in Taiwan. Because they are separated according to age groups, the 5-year-old groups in *yochien* and *youzhiyuan* are equivalent to the American kindergarten. Most kindergartens and preschools are privately owned in Japan and Taiwan, and attendance is optional. Even so, attendance is high. On the average, the Sendai children had spent more months in *yochien* (23 months) than the Minneapolis children spent in nursery schools, day-care centers, and/or kindergarten com-

TABLE 5

AVERAGE FIRST-GRADE READING AND MATHEMATICS SCORES OF CHILDREN WHO ATTENDED PRESCHOOL FOR VARYING AMOUNTS OF TIME

YEARS	UNITED STATES		TAIWAN		JAPAN	
	M	SD	M	SD	M	SD
Reading:						
Less than 1 year	...	...	17	15	...	...
1 year	15	14	20	14	16	13
2 years	22	18	25	19	19	12
3 years	24	20	27	18	16	10
F	4.54		3.55		1.53	
df	(2,198)		(3,230)		(2,233)	
p	.05		.05		N.S.	
Mathematics:						
Less than 1 year	...	...	24	9	...	...
1 year	22	7	27	6	25	6
2 years	23	8	30	6	27	7
3 years	25	6	29	7	25	7
F	2.33		7.43		2.02	
df	(2,198)		(3,230)		(2,233)	
p	N.S.		.001		N.S.	

bined (20 months). The Chinese children spent an average of 18 months in *youzhiyuan*. No Minneapolis children and very few of the Sendai children (1%) had spent less than a year in kindergarten; in Taipei, 19% of the children fell in this category.

The relation between length of preschool attendance and first-grade achievement in reading was positive in Taipei and Minneapolis but not in Sendai; for mathematics, the relation was significant only in Taipei (see Table 5). Because attendance at preschool is typically correlated with parents' education, we conducted regression analyses of the achievement data, including both amount of preschool education and mothers' education. Mothers' education contributed significantly in prediction of achievement in reading and mathematics, all p's $< .001$, except for Taiwan, $p < .05$. Length of preschool attendance was not a significant factor in either Minneapolis or Sendai, but it was in Taipei for both reading, partial $r = .15$, $p < .05$, and mathematics, partial $r = .20$, $p < .01$. The multiple R^2 obtained from the six analyses ranged from .26 to .32. In short, length of preschool experience did not improve the prediction of academic achievement in Sendai and Minneapolis, where mothers generally had a high school education, but it did improve prediction in Taipei, where the average maternal level of education was lower.

CONCLUDING COMMENTS

Although demographic characteristics of the families, what children know before they enter school, and extent of preschool experience often have been found to be significantly related to achievement, these variables proved to be of little help in understanding differences in achievement between the three cultures being studied. For example, Chinese children had parents with the least amounts of education, were estimated to have the least knowledge about reading before entering the first grade, and were the least likely to have attended kindergarten—yet they had the highest levels of reading achievement several months after they entered elementary school. Within each culture, however, these variables were, in general, significantly related to children's achievement. Paradoxically, variables such as years of parents' education—which offer likely explanations of differences in performance among children within a culture—do not necessarily prove to be useful in discussing cross-cultural differences in performance. Conversely, variables reflecting motivational differences that will be discussed varied directly with levels of achievement between cultures but did not covary with level of achievement within cultures. For example, American mothers, whose children obtained the lowest achievement scores in mathematics, placed the least emphasis on the importance of effort on achievement, while Japanese mothers, whose children obtained the highest scores, placed the most stress on effort. In sum, variables that predict differences in performance between cultures may not be the same variables as those that predict differences among individuals within a culture.

VI. CHILDREN'S LIVES AT HOME

USE OF TIME

Academic and nonacademic activities.—Mothers were asked to describe their child's activities on the day prior to the interview by first reporting when the child got up, went to school, came home, and went to bed. The mother then gave a detailed account of her child's activities after school. In terms of waking hours, the typical day for fifth graders in Minneapolis lasted 14.0 hours, in Taipei 15.2 hours, and in Sendai 14.7 hours. The typical day for first graders was approximately a half hour shorter in each city.

When asked to describe their child's after-school activities, more of the Chinese and Japanese than the American mothers mentioned activities related to academic pursuits (e.g., studying, reading, playing academically related games). On the other hand, the American mothers were more likely than the Chinese and Japanese mothers to describe nonacademic activities of their child, such as social interactions with friends and family members, watching television, sports, and extracurricular activities like music, dancing classes, and Girl and Boy Scouts (see Table 6).

Academic activities were mentioned by more mothers of fifth than of first graders in both Minneapolis and Sendai; in Taipei, a very high percentage of mothers mentioned these at both grades. Nearly all Minneapolis mothers mentioned nonacademic activities at both grades, but in the other two cities mothers were much less likely to note such activities if their child was in the fifth than if their child was in the first grade.

Greater involvement of Chinese children in academic activities and of American children in nonacademic activities was also evident when mothers were asked to estimate the amounts of time their child had spent in homework, play, and watching television on the previous weekday, Saturday, and Sunday. The weekday estimates were multiplied by five and added to the estimates for Saturday and Sunday to provide estimates for a full week. Estimates of how much time the child spent reading for pleasure

TABLE 6

PERCENTAGE OF MOTHERS MENTIONING ACADEMIC (A) AND NONACADEMIC (NA) AFTER-SCHOOL ACTIVITIES: PERCENTAGE OF CHILDREN WHO SAY THEY ENJOY THESE ACTIVITIES

	United States		Taiwan		Japan	
	A	NA	A	NA	A	NA
Mothers:						
Grade 1 ..	47	99	85	73	74	93
Grade 5 ..	68	96	89	38	85	55
Children:						
Grade 1 ..	5	79	84	61	21	85
Grade 5 ..	18	76	69	52	24	73

during the previous week were also obtained. The estimates are shown in Table 7.

The mothers estimated that Chinese children spent about four times as much time each day doing homework as the American children and over twice as much as the Japanese children. Differences were as dramatic at the first grade as they were at the fifth.

TABLE 7

TIME SPENT ON PLAY, WATCHING TELEVISION, READING FOR PLEASURE, AND HOMEWORK (in Hours)

	United States	Taiwan	Japan	F	Scheffé Contrasts
Grade 1:					
Play	22.1	12.5	21.8	80.27	U & J > T
	(8.5)	(8.1)	(8.3)	[.001]	[.001]
Television	12.8	11.3	15.1	25.73	J > U > T
	(5.9)	(5.5)	(6.0)	[.001]	[.001] [.05]
Reading for pleasure	3.1	3.9	5.0	13.97	J > T; J > U
	(3.0)	(3.5)	(4.6)	[.001]	[.05] [.001]
Homework	1.2	8.2	3.9	264.16	T > J > U
	(1.7)	(4.7)	(2.4)	[.001]	[.001] [.001]
Grade 5:					
Play	20.2	8.1	14.1	115.73	U > J > T
	(9.4)	(5.5)	(7.2)	[.001]	[.001] [.001]
Television	14.2	10.6	16.0	49.61	J > U > T
	(6.6)	(4.6)	(6.2)	[.001]	[.01] [.001]
Reading for pleasure	4.5	4.8	6.4	15.15	J > U & T
	(3.9)	(3.6)	(4.4)	[.001]	[.001]
Homework	4.2	12.9	6.0	205.11	T > J > U
	(3.6)	(6.5)	(3.5)	[.001]	[.001] [.05]

NOTE.—Standard deviations are given in parentheses and p levels in brackets. df's = 2,608–676 (grade 1); 2,601–672 (grade 5).

The Japanese children also spent more time reading for pleasure than did the American and Chinese children. Again, cross-cultural differences were as great at the first as at the fifth grade. The American and Japanese children spent much more time than the Chinese children playing. Time devoted to play declined moderately between the first and the fifth grades for the American children but much more strongly for the Chinese and Japanese children. Japanese children watched more television each week than the American children, who, in turn, watched more television than the Chinese children.

Mothers and children differed in all three cities in the salience they accorded television. Children did not describe television viewing as something they especially enjoyed doing after school; mothers, on the other hand, frequently mentioned it among their child's after-school activities. The percentage of mothers and of children mentioning television was as follows: 73% versus 37% in Minneapolis; 60% versus 42% in Taipei; and 93% versus 11% in Sendai. These data suggest that children may turn to television more because it is routinely available than because it is especially attractive.

Two activities that characterized the American more than the Chinese and Japanese families were children's chores and parent-child interaction. In Minneapolis, 34% of the mothers said that their child had chores to do after school. Only 6% of the Taipei and 9% of the Japanese mothers mentioned chores; their most common reason for not assigning chores was that these divert children from their schoolwork. Parent-child interaction—which included interaction outside mealtimes and discussions of school activities—was mentioned by 42% of the American mothers but by only 1% of the Chinese and 13% of the Japanese mothers. It is hard to know whether this reflects a lower level of social interaction between these mothers and their children or whether such interactions occur so automatically that they were not perceived as being salient.

Children's preferences for after-school activities.—Children's answers to what they liked to do after school were also classified into academic and nonacademic activities (see Table 6). Many more of the Chinese than of the American or Japanese children spontaneously described academic or cognitive activities, such as after-school classes, lessons, schoolwork, doing puzzles, playing chess, or reading. Conversely, more of the American and Japanese children mentioned nonacademic activities. Many more of the mothers than of the children in Minneapolis mentioned academic activities. The same pattern appeared in the Sendai families, but responses of the Taipei mothers and their children were in closer accord.

It seems reasonable to conclude that Chinese children not only were the most likely to engage in academic activities after school but also seemed to gain the most enjoyment from them. Japanese children engaged in academic activities but did not often describe these activities as something they enjoyed doing. American children, however, were less likely to undertake academic activities after school, and they apparently did not find the time they spent especially enjoyable.

ACADEMIC EXPERIENCES OUT OF SCHOOL

After-school classes and tutoring.—More children in Sendai (15%) than in Taipei (about 2%) or Minneapolis (about 10%) were enrolled in nonremedial after-school academic classes or had a tutor for academic subjects. Among Japanese children, after-school academic classes were attended by 16% of the first graders and 46% of the fifth graders. However, most of these classes were devoted to the study of English or the use of the abacus rather than to reading or mathematics. Only 10% of the children studied mathematics; in the other two cities, fewer than 6% studied either reading or mathematics. Attendance at after-school academic classes had no relation to academic achievement in any of the three cities.

In contrast to the low frequency of attendance at after-school academic classes, 67% of the Minneapolis children participated in nonacademic classes, such as sports, music, and art; the corresponding values were 30% for Taipei and 53% for Sendai. Thus, what differed among the three cities was not the percentage of children enrolled in after-school classes but the type of classes in which the children were enrolled.

Homework.—Homework merits special attention in any discussion of out-of-school academic activities since the extra practice afforded by homework may be an important factor in affecting level of academic achievement. In addition to asking mothers to estimate the time their child spent on homework during the preceding week, we asked the teachers to estimate the length of time required to complete the homework assigned on the day they responded to the question. The American first-grade teachers estimated that the daily homework assignment would require an average of 3 min; the estimates offered by the Chinese and Japanese teachers were 40 and 15 min, respectively. For fifth graders, the teachers' estimates increased to 20 min in Minneapolis, 78 min in Taipei, and 37 min in Sendai. These estimates are lower than those of the mothers but are in the same relative order.

Homework assignments were not limited to the times school was in session. All the Chinese teachers reported giving their pupils homework to complete during their winter vacation. This vacation corresponds to the Western Christmas vacation, during which only 12% of the Minneapolis teachers gave their pupils homework to complete. In Japan, where the school year begins in April, 68% of the teachers made homework assign-

TABLE 8

CHILDREN'S ATTITUDES TOWARD HOMEWORK

	United States	Taiwan	Japan	F	Scheffé Contrasts
Grade 1	2.5	3.8	3.2	63.22	T > J > U
	(1.5)	(1.1)	(1.3)	[.001]	[.001] [.001]
Grade 5	2.2	3.6	2.8	133.61	T > J > U
	(1.1)	(1.0)	(.8)	[.001]	[.001] [.001]
Grade 5, follow-up[a] ...	2.4	3.6	2.7	63.81	T > J > U
	(.9)	(1.0)	(.9)	[.001]	[.001] [.01]

NOTE.—Standard deviations are given in parentheses and p levels in brackets. df's = 2,713 (grade 1); 2,721 (grade 5); 2,443 (grade 5, follow-up). Scales range from 1 ("dislike very much") to 5 ("like very much").

[a] The seven-point scale was transformed into a five-point scale here for purposes of comparison.

ments during the 6-week summer break, the longest vacation within the school year.

Children in the three cultures had very different responses to doing homework (see Table 8). Children in Minneapolis did not like homework; Taipei children liked homework; and the attitudes of Sendai children were more neutral. The long hours devoted to homework by Chinese children did not reduce their enthusiasm: they were nearly as positive about homework at the fifth grade as they were at the first.

The children's reactions to homework reflect, in part, attitudes of their teachers and parents. Teachers rated how strongly they believed homework to be of value to children. American teachers apparently were not convinced that homework is of great help. In each instance, American teachers were less positive about homework than were Chinese or Japanese teachers. As can be seen in Table 9, Chinese teachers were the most convinced that homework was of value.

TABLE 9

TEACHER'S RATINGS OF THF VALUE OF HOMEWORK IN VARIOUS SUBJECTS

	United States	Taiwan	Japan	F	Scheffé Contrasts
Reading	5.4	7.0	5.8	4.37	T > U
	(2.6)	(1.8)	(2.4)	[.05]	[.05]
Mathematics	5.4	7.1	6.2	5.72	T > U
	(2.6)	(1.6)	(1.9)	[.01]	[.01]
Spelling	5.4	7.8	7.1	10.89	T > U; J > U
	(2.7)	(1.4)	(2.0)	[.001]	[.001] [.01]
Social studies	3.3	6.6	5.0	22.26	T > J > U
	(2.0)	(1.4)	(2.2)	[.001]	[.01] [.01]

NOTE.—Standard deviations are given in parentheses and p levels in brackets. df = 2,96–100. Scales ranged from 1 ("of little help") to 9 ("of great help").

Reading for pleasure.—Children's newspapers and children's pages in newspapers for adults are much more accessible to children in Taiwan, where newspapers are inexpensive and available in most classrooms, than in Japan or the United States. In Taipei, 56% of the children read newspapers, compared to 24% in Minneapolis and 31% in Sendai. On the average, Japanese families subscribed to 1.2 children's magazines, versus .9 in Minneapolis and .5 in Taipei.

Comic books (*manhua* in Chinese, *manga* in Japanese) have a special role for readers of Chinese and Japanese. Taipei and Sendai children spent more than one-third of their time devoted to reading for pleasure reading comic books. Although the story may sometimes be complex, comic books consist primarily of drawings with minimal text. Few Minneapolis children read comics (4%) or magazines (12%); their reading was most likely to be devoted to books (77%).

STUDY ENVIRONMENT AT HOME

Homes and apartments in Japan and Taiwan are much smaller than those in the United States, and allocation of any space within the home for activities of a single individual occurs at a cost to the total family. Nevertheless, over 80% of the families provided their child with a quiet place to study. Purchase of a personal desk is also indicative of the importance families place on providing their child with a satisfactory place to work on school-related tasks. Only 63% of the American fifth graders but 95% of the Chinese and 98% of the Japanese fifth graders had their own desk. Even in the first grade, fewer American (67%) than Chinese (83%) or Japanese (91%) children had their own desk.

Workbooks provide another opportunity for children to practice what they have learned in school and to acquire new information and skills. Especially in Japan, workbooks are featured in department stores, book shops, and neighborhood newsstands. These books are full of exercises, games, and puzzles aimed at enhancing the children's understanding of their schoolwork, and inexpensive editions are published separately by grade and topic. In Taipei, workbooks are also readily available; however, in American cities, such an array of books is relatively hard to find (other than those stocked by grocery stores and featured in some bookstores). The purchase of workbooks by the Minneapolis mothers declined between the first and the fifth grade from 61% to 41%. In contrast, the percentage increased in Taipei (28%–67%) and Sendai (56%–61%). Most of the workbooks purchased in all three cities were for reading or mathematics, but a much higher percentage of the workbooks purchased in Taipei and Sendai than in Minneapolis were in science (52%, 41%, and 2%, respectively, at the first grade;

83%, 48%, and 4% at the fifth grade). It appears, therefore, that the supplementary assistance provided by responding to workbooks was less prevalent in Minneapolis than in the other two cities.

CONCLUDING COMMENTS

Elementary school children in Minneapolis, Taipei, and Sendai allocated their time in different ways. These differences appear to us to offer one reasonable explanation of the high academic performance of Chinese and Japanese children: they worked longer, and presumably harder, on their schoolwork.

Children's everyday lives in Taipei and Sendai were oriented toward academic activities. This was not the case in Minneapolis, where academic activities did not appear to have the same significance for the children, who tended to spend their time engaged in activities that may lead to other accomplishments, but not those in academic areas. The American children spent their out-of-school hours playing, being engaged in social interaction with friends and family, taking lessons in nonacademic subjects, and doing chores. Although the Chinese and Japanese children also played and watched television, they nevertheless were much more likely to be involved in academic activities after school. American parents were tolerant, therefore, of their children's spending large amounts of time in activities that they believed would make them into well-rounded individuals. Chinese and Japanese parents, in contrast, appeared to believe that the route to future happiness is through high academic success, and, as long as their child studies diligently, they were willing to be lenient in other aspects of their child's life.

The cross-cultural differences in the scholastic achievement of elementary school children cannot be attributed to the pervasive use of supplementary forms of education from sources outside the home. Few of the children participated in cram schools or after-school lessons dealing directly with academic work. The primary function of these after-school classes in Taiwan and Japan is to prepare older students for entrance examinations to high schools and college. Nor can the performance of the Japanese children be credited to mothers who supplemented their schoolwork with intensive drill and instruction. These after-school activities may be phenomena found in later years of school, but they do not characterize the elementary school years of either Japanese or Chinese children.

VII. CHILDREN'S ATTITUDES

ATTITUDES ABOUT SCHOOL

Our explorations of children's attitudes about school consistently led to the same results: the Chinese children liked school the most; the American and Japanese children were less positive. Between 75% and 86% (according to grade and study) of the Chinese children, compared to between 52% and 65% of the American children, indicated that they liked school. Of the Japanese children, 64% in the follow-up study said they liked school. (This item was not included in the initial interviews with the Japanese children.) The mothers, however, had a different opinion about their child's attitudes. More than 90% of the American and Chinese mothers believed that their child liked school, but 74% of the Japanese mothers held this belief. The discrepancy between ratings made by the child and by the mother was obviously greater in the American than in the Chinese and Japanese families.[3]

Although they differed in level, ratings made by the mothers and the children were positively related to each other, r's = .37, .23, and .24 in Minneapolis, Taipei, and Sendai, all p's < .01. Thus, even though the mothers tended to exaggerate their child's liking for school—particularly in Minneapolis—they still displayed an awareness of their child's feelings.

One way of understanding what it means to like school is to consider the relation between children's ratings of how well they liked school and of how well they liked reading and mathematics. This was done for the fifth graders in the follow-up study. In Minneapolis, the correlation was .03 with mathematics but .36 with reading—a significant difference, $t(232) = 2.66, p < .01$. In contrast, how well Chinese and Japanese children liked school was significantly related to how well they liked both mathematics and reading, p's < .01. (Correlations for Taipei were .38 and .23 and for Sendai .27 and .42.)

---

[3] In this and other instances of severely skewed distributions, we report the results in terms of percentage of subjects above or below the midpoint of the distributions (i.e., percentage of ratings above or below the "neutral" point).

Children's feelings about school were also evaluated by asking the first and fifth graders to complete the sentence, "School is ———." Answers were categorized into five levels, ranging from strongly positive to strongly negative. The Japanese children held similar attitudes at both grades: positive feelings (levels 4 and 5) were expressed by 52% of the first and 53% of the fifth graders. However, the American children were less positive in the fifth grade than in the first, whereas the Chinese children became more positive at the fifth than at the first grade: between grades 1 and 5, the percentage declined from 69% to 44% in Minneapolis but increased from 10% to 43% in Taipei. In general, the Chinese and Japanese children were more likely to express positive attitudes about school in their ratings than in their spontaneous comments, but the general reactions of the American children were similar for the two types of responses.

Negative (e.g., boring, dull) or strongly negative responses (e.g., terrible, horrible, stupid) were made by 11% of the American children, less than 1% of the Chinese children, and 3% of the Japanese children. Neutral responses (e.g., fine, okay) were made by 24% of the American, 72% of the Chinese, and 43% of the Japanese children.

Another index of children's reactions to school was obtained from mothers' reports about their child's refusals to attend school. Mothers were told:

> Young children sometimes don't want to go to school. Suppose ——— gets up one morning and says, "I *won't* go to school today!" You know that ——— is not sick. Has this ever happened?

More Minneapolis mothers reported instances of such refusals (50%) than did Taipei (11%) or Sendai (26%) mothers, indicating not only that the American children were less prone to report liking school but also that many of them had expressed this dislike at one time or another by not wanting to go to school.

ATTITUDES ABOUT READING AND MATHEMATICS

In their ratings of how well they liked reading and mathematics, the majority of children in all three cities expressed neutral or positive attitudes. Minneapolis first graders liked reading better than mathematics, but those in Taipei and Sendai liked both subjects equally well. In the initial study, children in the fifth grade in all three cities liked reading better than mathematics. In the follow-up study, American fifth graders were the most enthusiastic about mathematics and the Chinese fifth graders were the most enthusiastic about reading (see Table 10). (Questions for the American

TABLE 10

Children's Ratings of How Much They Liked Mathematics and Reading

	United States	Taiwan	Japan	F	Scheffé Contrasts
Grade 1:					
Mathematics	3.3	3.7	3.7	7.05	T & J > U
	(1.4)	(1.2)	(1.2)	[.001]	[.01]
Reading	3.9	3.8	3.7	1.65	...
	(1.3)	(1.2)	(1.1)	[N.S.]	
Grade 5:					
Mathematics	3.3	3.3	3.2	.62	...
	(1.4)	(1.3)	(1.0)	[N.S.]	
Reading	3.6	4.0	3.7	10.72	T > U; T > J
	(1.2)	(.9)	(1.0)	[.001]	[.001] [.01]
Grade 5, follow-up:[a]					
Mathematics	3.9	3.5	3.2	10.82	U > T; U > J
	(1.3)	(1.2)	(1.2)	[.001]	[.05] [.001]
Reading	3.1	4.1	3.3	45.00	T > U & J
	(1.1)	(.9)	(1.0)	[.001]	[.001]

Note.—Standard deviations are given in parentheses and p levels in brackets. df's = 2,713–714 (grade 1); 2,721 (grade 5); 2,444 (grade 5, follow-up). Scales range from 1 ("very little") to 5 ("very much").

[a] The seven-point scale was transformed into a five-point scale here for purposes of comparison.

children in the follow-up study were phrased in terms of "English [language arts]" rather than "reading"; they were told that, "when we say language arts, we mean reading, writing, and spelling." The questions were asked in terms of *kokugo* for Japanese and *guoyu* in Chinese; both terms mean "national language.")

How much children liked mathematics was related to their performance on the mathematics achievement test in both grades and in all three locations, r's = .15–.46, p's < .05. In the case of reading, the relation was significant in all three locations for first graders, r's = .13–.24, p's < .05, but was significant for fifth graders only in Sendai in the initial study, r = .30, p < .001, and in Minneapolis in the follow-up study, r = .18, p < .05.

SELF-EVALUATIONS OF ABILITIES

Intelligence.—Children in the follow-up study were asked where they would place themselves if they were to rank all the students in their class "from the brightest to the most stupid." The mean self-ratings made by Minneapolis children were significantly higher than those made in Taipei and Sendai (see Table 11).

Children's self-ratings of brightness can be used to clarify the perception of reading and mathematics in the three cultures. The American children's self-perceptions of their brightness were strongly related to their

TABLE 11

CHILDREN'S EVALUATION OF THEIR ABILITIES

	United States	Taiwan	Japan	F	Scheffé Contrasts
Intelligence (brightness)[a]	4.9	4.2	4.0	21.10	U > T & J
	(1.1)	(1.2)	(1.0)	[.001]	[.001]
Schoolwork[b]	4.6	4.3	3.9	10.60	U > J; T > J
	(1.1)	(1.3)	(1.1)	[.001]	[.001] [.01]
Mathematics[c]	5.0	4.3	4.2	11.24	U > T & J
	(1.4)	(1.4)	(1.7)	[.001]	[.001]
Reading[d]	4.8	5.1	4.2	24.02	U & T > J
	(1.2)	(1.1)	(1.4)	[.001]	[.001]
Potential for achievement[e]	5.7	5.4	4.8	14.83	U & T > J
	(1.5)	(1.6)	(1.3)	[.001]	[.001]

NOTE.—Standard deviations are given in parentheses and p levels in brackets. df = 2,442–444.

[a] "If you were to rank all the students in your class from the brightest to the most stupid, where would you put yourself?" (1 = "the most stupid," 7 = "the brightest").

[b] "If you were to rank all the students in your class from the worst to the best in schoolwork, where would you put yourself?" (1 = "the worst," 7 = "the best").

[c] "How good at math are you?" (1 = "not at all good," 7 = "very good").

[d] "How good are you at language arts (reading)?" (1 = "not at all good," 7 = "very good").

[e] "If you work your hardest, could you be among the best students in your class?" (1 = "absolutuely impossible," 7 = "absolutely possible").

evaluations of their reading ability. The Japanese children were more likely to consider themselves to be bright if they perceived themselves as being skilled in mathematics. For the American children, the correlation between self-ratings of brightness and their evaluation of their own abilities was .47 for reading and .20 for mathematics, a significant difference, $t(236) = 2.36$, $p < .05$. The comparable correlations did not differ significantly for the Chinese children, r's = .31 and .39, but did differ for the Japanese children, r's = .16 and .46, $t(326) = 3.05, p < .01$.

School achievement.—The children rated themselves on how well they were doing in their schoolwork. Again, Minneapolis children gave themselves the highest ratings (see Table 11). To evaluate whether these self-evaluations were more strongly related to one subject than the other, correlations were computed with their ratings of their own skill in mathematics and reading. The greater influence of mathematics than of reading was again evident in the ratings made by the Chinese and Japanese children. The correlations were .55 for mathematics and .25 for reading in Taipei, $t(322) = 3.08, p < .01$, and .47 versus .25 in Sendai, $t(326) = 2.29, p < .05$. In Minneapolis, both correlations were .41.

The self-evaluations of performance in mathematics and reading placed Sendai fifth graders near the average for both subjects; in Taipei, children rated themselves near average for mathematics but were more positive about their reading ability. Minneapolis children gave themselves high ratings in both subjects (see Table 11).

Despite these mean differences, correlations between ratings of how good the children believed they were in mathematics and their scores on the mathematics achievement test were similar for the American (.41), Chinese (.46), and Japanese children (.49), all p's < .001. Evaluating their own reading ability proved to be more difficult, especially for the Japanese children; correlations between their self-ratings and their reading scores were .36, p's < .01, for both American and Chinese children but only .05 for Japanese children. It is not clear why the latter correlation was so remarkably low. Perhaps it is related to the fact noted earlier that four writing systems must be mastered in learning to read in Japan. Ability to read one system is not necessarily related to ability to read another, and children may find it confusing to evaluate their overall reading ability.

When asked, "If you worked your hardest, could you be among the best students in your class?" American and Chinese children believed that it was possible; Japanese children were less sure (see Table 11). The correlations between ratings made by children of their potential for schoolwork and the summary score for achievement were .36 (Minneapolis), .49 (Taipei), and .23 (Sendai), all p's < .01.

Relations between achievement and attitudes.—Some of the strongest correlations obtained in the study were between the children's ratings of how good they thought they were in a subject and how much they liked the subject. For reading, the correlations were .55, .40, and .68 for the American, Chinese, and Japanese children. For mathematics, the correlations were even higher, .58, .61, and .77. Children clearly liked the subjects in which they thought they were doing well and disliked subjects in which they thought they were doing poorly.

Why did American children like mathematics and believe that they were good at it? The answer seems to be that mathematics curricula in the United States are easier than those of Asian countries. Some evidence for this point appeared in the fifth graders' ratings of the difficulty of mathematics. American and Chinese children rated mathematics as significantly less difficult than did the Japanese children, $F(2,444) = 5.24, p < .01; J > T$ and U, p's < .05. The mean ratings were 3.5, 3.6, and 4.0, respectively. Analyses of the mathematics textbooks used in the three locations also indicate that mathematical concepts tend to be introduced somewhat earlier in Japanese than in American textbooks (Stevenson & Bartsch, in press).

PERCEPTIONS OF PARENTS' AND TEACHERS' SATISFACTION

Children's perceptions of how well they were doing in school were also reflected in their ratings of how satisfied they thought their parents and teachers were with their achievement. When asked if they were doing as well

TABLE 12

PREDICTION OF CHILDREN'S ACADEMIC SELF-CONCEPT FROM THEIR
ACHIEVEMENT SCORES AND THEIR PERCEPTIONS OF PARENTS' AND TEACHERS'
SATISFACTION WITH THEIR SCHOOLWORK

	BETA		
	United States	Taiwan	Japan
Achievement scores	.46***	.54***	.34***
Parent satisfaction	.21*	.02	.06
Teacher satisfaction	.09	.14	.25**
N	115	154	161
R^2	.35	.30	.24

* $p > .05$.
** $p > .01$.
*** $p > .001$.

in their schoolwork as their parents and teachers wanted them to, American children were more convinced than Chinese and Japanese children that they were meeting these expectations. The average ratings on a seven-point scale of satisfaction were 4.9, 4.2, and 4.0 for the American, Chinese, and Japanese children when the question was asked about the parents' expectations, $F(2,441) = 12.70$, $p < .001$. A similar order was found when the children were asked about how happy their teacher was with their performance: the mean ratings were 4.8, 4.0, and 3.6 for the American, Chinese, and Japanese children, respectively, $F(2,441) = 26.15$, $p < .001$.

Children's ratings of their parents' and teachers' satisfaction with their academic performance may be related to their perceptions about how well they thought they were doing in school. These two variables, along with the child's summary achievement score, were used in regression analyses to predict the children's ratings of how well they believed they were doing in school. Minneapolis children's ratings of their academic achievement were significantly related to their actual academic achievement and to their perceptions about how satisfied their parents were with their performance; in Taipei, these were predicted solely by their scores on the achievement tests; and in Sendai, they were predicted both by achievement scores and ratings of their teacher's satisfaction (see Table 12).

MOTIVATION FOR GOING TO SCHOOL

In addition to categorizing the children's responses in completing the sentence, "School is ———," according to whether they liked school, we also categorized them in terms of academic activities (e.g., "a fun place to learn"), social activities (e.g., "a place to meet new people"), or play (e.g., "where I can play"). Children's responses could, of course, be incorporated in more than one of these categories. Taipei children frequently mentioned academic activities—76%, compared to 32% of the Minneapolis children and 23% of the Sendai children. Less than 12% of the children in any location mentioned the social aspects of elementary school, but more Chinese (34%) than American (3%) or Japanese children (5%) mentioned play. In Minneapolis, 74% of the children completed the sentence most frequently with an affective response, such as "terrific," "kinda good," "boring," "bad," or "terrible." Such responses were made by 25% of the Chinese and 56% of the Japanese children.

A more direct approach to tapping children's conceptions of the functions of school is to ask them why they go to school and why they study. Fifth graders were asked to rate four alternatives that completed the phrase, "I spend as much time doing schoolwork as I do because ———," and six reasons "for coming to school." Factor analyses of these ratings performed separately for each location yielded the same three factors in each city. The strength of the factor loadings of the items differed somewhat in the three cultures, but in each case there were three distinct factors. The first factor reflected the child's interest in learning, the second emphasis on external forces, and the third social aspects of school. The factors were labeled "internal," "external," and "social orientation"; items included in each factor and item means for each city appear in Table 13.

The strongest external orientation characterized the American children, and the strongest internal orientation was among the Chinese children. Ratings for the third factor, social orientation, did not differ significantly among the three groups of children (see Table 14).

The Minneapolis children's greater dependency on parental sources of motivation can be seen in the ratings that they assigned to the two alternatives involving parental pressure (see Table 13). They considered the desires of their parents to be relatively more important in matters such as going to school and carrying out schoolwork than did the children in Sendai or Taipei.

WORRIES ABOUT SCHOOLWORK

It has been suggested by critics of Chinese and Japanese educational systems that one of the costs of the pressure they exert for achievement is emotional disturbance among children. We saw no evidence of this during our classroom observations; children in all three cultures appeared to be cheerful, enthusiastic, vigorous, and responsive. The children appeared to be happy, and this was evident in their ratings of how happy they were in comparison to other children in their class. The average ratings on a seven-

TABLE 13

ITEMS INCLUDED IN THE INTERNAL, EXTERNAL, AND SOCIAL ORIENTATION FACTORS

	Internal	External	Social
I spend as much time doing schoolwork as I do because	I like doing it. (3.6, 4.0, 3.1)	It takes me that much time in order to finish. (4.6, 3.2, 3.7)	
		My parents want me to. (4.1, 2.3, 3.0)	
		I don't want to be punished by the teacher. (3.8, 4.1, 2.7)	
I come to school because	I like the subjects we study. (4.8, 5.6, 3.6)	My parents want me to. (5.2, 4.3, 2.0)	I like to see my friends there. (5.1, 4.5, 5.1)
	I can learn many useful things from school. (6.2, 6.3, 4.7)	Students have to. (5.4, 4.7, 3.7)	I like the special activities we do there, like sports and band. (5.4, 5.2, 4.9)

NOTE.—The item means appear in parentheses in the order United States, Taiwan, and Japan. The scales range from 1 ("not very true") to 7 ("very true").

point scale for the American, Chinese, and Japanese children were high: 5.2, 5.3, and 4.8, respectively, $F(2,444) = 5.32$, $p < .01$, U and T > J, p's < .05.

To check further on whether our observations were in accord with the children's feelings, we asked the fifth graders in the follow-up study to answer a number of questions about possible sources of worry and concern

TABLE 14

MEAN RATINGS OF IMPORTANCE OF SOURCES OF MOTIVATION

	United States	Taiwan	Japan	F	Scheffé Contrasts
Internal	4.9	5.3	3.8	75.81	T > U > J
	(1.0)	(1.2)	(1.2)	[.001]	[.01] [.001]
External	4.6	3.7	3.0	57.63	U > T > J
	(1.0)	(1.3)	(.9)	[.001]	[.001] [.001]
Social	5.2	4.8	5.0	2.78	...
	(1.3)	(1.2)	(1.4)	[N.S.]	

NOTE.—Standard deviations are given in parentheses and p levels in brackets. $df = 2,444$.

TABLE 15

Mean Ratings Assigned by Fifth Graders to Possible Sources of Worries

	United States	Taiwan[a]	Japan	F	Scheffé Contrasts
Nervous when taking tests[b]	4.2 (1.7)	...	3.4 (1.8)	14.48 [.001]	U > J [.001]
Getting schoolwork done in time[c]	4.5 (1.8)	...	3.9 (1.9)	7.23 [.01]	U > J [.01]
Nervous when getting back grades[d]	4.1 (1.9)	...	4.0 (2.0)	.04 [N.S.]	...
Afraid of lagging behind[e]	3.8 (1.7)	6.3 (1.1)	4.7 (2.0)	83.00 [.001]	T > J > U [.001] [.001]
Afraid of not following teacher[f]	3.9 (1.7)	5.9 (1.5)	4.8 (1.7)	54.29 [.001]	T > J > U [.001] [.001]

Note.—Standard deviations are given in parentheses and p levels in brackets. df's = 1,280–281 (rows 1–3); 2,442 (rows 4 and 5). Scales range from 1 ("never") to 5 ("often").

[a] The first three items were omitted in Taiwan.
[b] "While you are taking a test how nervous do you get?"
[c] "How worried do you get about getting your schoolwork in on time?"
[d] "How nervous do you get when the teacher hands back grades on class assignments?"
[e] "If you are absent from school for a few days, how much do you worry that you will be behind other students when you come back to school?"
[f] "How much do you worry that you will not be able to follow what the teacher teaches in class?"

(see Table 15). The American children rated themselves as being more nervous than did the Japanese children while taking a test and expressed more worry about getting their schoolwork in on time.

There were two other questions about the children's worries, but in these cases the questions dealt with the children's concern about progress in school. Taipei children expressed the greatest concern and Minneapolis children the least (see Table 15).

To evaluate the children's worry about grades, they were asked about how upset their parents and their teachers would be if they got a low grade on an important test. The Japanese children were least worried: 44% of the Japanese but only 16% of the American and 10% of the Chinese children thought that their parents would not be very upset (i.e., chose 1 on a seven-point scale). Japanese children also thought that their teachers would not be upset. The percentages of children who thought their teachers would not be very upset were 65% (Japanese), 28% (American), and 4% (Chinese).

CONCLUDING COMMENTS

Critics of Chinese and Japanese education often suggest that the high demands placed on children in Asian schools result in ambivalent feelings or actual dislike of school. This does not seem to be the case at the elementary school level. American children were the ones who regarded elementary school less positively. American children's attitudes cannot be derived from being in school too long or having to work too hard while they are there. Their classes are small, and teachers do not assign large amounts of homework. The schools are not crowded, bleak, or uncomfortable. American children's expressions of dislike for school must reflect, in part, their belief that school is not an interesting place to be. The picture is different in Taiwan. Education is highly prized in the Chinese culture, a situation that must give children a sense of purpose, accomplishment, and pleasure as they work hard and strive to achieve in their schoolwork. Large classes, crowded schools, long hours in school, and large amounts of homework do not necessarily result in a dislike for school when gaining an education is considered to be one of the paramount accomplishments in life and when the school day and classroom learning are organized to be interesting.

The American children did not especially like school; nevertheless, they believed that they were doing well in school, that they were meeting the expectations of their parents and teachers, and that they were bright students with high potential for academic work. These beliefs help clarify why they were academically less successful than the Asian children. The very high self-perceptions and high confidence of the American children may prevent them from acknowledging the need to work hard. We also think that these children's tendency to define success more in terms of their performance in reading than in terms of their performance in mathematics offers insight into why their performance in mathematics was especially unimpressive.

Speculations about the possible negative effects of a strong emphasis on academic activities were not supported. There was no evidence that Chinese and Japanese elementary school children experienced more stress than their American counterparts. Instead, the Chinese children appeared to develop strong internal motivation toward learning and achievement.

Whatever the outcomes of the elementary school years in Japan, they do not appear to produce children who are worried about the responses of their parents or teachers to the possibility that they might not do well on an important test. Japanese mothers have been likened to good coaches, individuals who guide the players but keep cool under stress. Perhaps Japanese mothers and teachers do not show how upset they are when children do not do well in school because they believe that their children should be guided by their own sense of guilt about not performing effectively.

VIII. BELIEFS ABOUT EFFORT AND ABILITY

One of the most pervasive beliefs in Asian cultures is that effort is the major avenue for improvement and accomplishment. The malleability of human behavior has long been emphasized in Chinese writings and is one of the fundamental precepts of Confucianism (Munro, 1977). A typical example of this view is found in the writings of the Chinese philosopher Hsun Tzu, who wrote, "Achievement consists of never giving up. . . . If there is no dark and dogged will, there will be no shining accomplishment; if there is no dull and determined effort, there will be no brilliant achievement" (Watson, 1967, p. 18). According to this view, differences among individuals are believed to be primarily a result of life experiences rather than of innate differences.

A similar theme is found in Japanese philosophy, where individual differences in potential are deemphasized and great importance is placed on the role of effort in modifying the course of human development. Japanese values are summarized in the phrase, *Yareba dekiru* (If you try hard, you can do it). Effort and self-discipline are considered to be essential for accomplishment. Lack of achievement is attributed to the failure to work with utmost self-exertion rather than to a lack of ability or to personal or environmental obstacles. In many classrooms in Japan, one finds four written precepts that describe the ideal student; the first is *gambaru kodomo*—a child who strives his or her hardest.

MOTHERS' BELIEFS

Effort and ability.—The concepts of effort and ability have been widely used in psychological analyses of the academic motivation of American and other Western children and seemed likely to be important in understanding differences in the motivation of the children and of the mothers we studied. Among the few comparative studies of beliefs about effort and ability is that of Azuma et al. (1981), who reported that Tokyo mothers of preschool children placed greater emphasis on the value of effort than did their California counterparts and that their American mothers placed greater emphasis on ability than their Japanese mothers. We sought further evidence about the relative emphasis on effort and ability in the beliefs of Chinese, Japanese, and American mothers and their children in an attempt to determine whether the strength of these beliefs paralleled differences in children's achievement.

We investigated cultural differences in mothers' beliefs about the relative importance of effort and ability in many different ways. Our first method was to ask mothers first to rank order four factors—effort, natural ability, difficulty of schoolwork, and luck or chance—in terms of their relative importance and then to apportion 10 points among these. One point was to be assigned to the least important and the remainder split according to their relative importance. The literal meanings of the Chinese words used in our questions, *nuli* and *tiansheng nengli*, were, respectively, (child's) effort and the ability one is born with. The Japanese words *doryoku* and *umaretsuki noryoku* mean one's own effort and the natural ability one is born with. We believe the concepts thus were very comparable in the three languages.

Rank orders of the importance of the items were the same in all three cultures; however, the relative emphasis given to effort and ability, the two factors of greatest interest to us, differed significantly. The mean number of points assigned to each of the items by the mothers in each culture are presented in Table 16. For comparisons of effort and ability, we subtracted the number of the points mothers assigned to ability from those they assigned to effort. The mean difference was small in Minneapolis (.51), larger for Taipei (1.77), and quite large for Sendai (2.71), $F(2,1317) = 76.63$, $p < .001$, J > T > U, p's < .001. In other words, the emphasis given to effort relative to ability is much higher among Japanese and Chinese mothers than among American mothers. American mothers gave only a slightly greater emphasis to effort than to ability. (Because the differences were as strong among mothers of first graders as among mothers of fifth graders, the data were combined for Table 16.)

Several other attempts to probe beliefs about the role of effort and ability in children's achievement were included in the interview held with the mothers in the follow-up study. The mothers rated their agreement with a number of statements related to ability and effort. It is evident in Table 17 that the Japanese mothers were most likely to agree that children tend to have the same amount of ability in reading and mathematics but that the American mothers were most likely to agree that chidren were born with these abilities. Conversely, Japanese mothers were more likely to believe that any child could be good at reading or mathematics if he or she worked hard enough (see Table 17).

Parents who believe that all children have equal amounts of natural

TABLE 16

Average Points Mothers Assigned to the Importance of Ability, Effort, Task Difficulty, and Luck in Determining Children's School Performance

	United States	Taiwan	Japan	F	Scheffé Contrasts
Effort	3.9	4.4	5.1	67.96	J > T > U
	(1.3)	(1.4)	(2.0)	[.001]	[.001] [.001]
Ability	3.4	2.6	2.4	55.03	U > T & J
	(1.2)	(1.1)	(1.6)	[.001]	[.001]
Task difficulty	1.9	1.9	1.4	37.63	U & T > J
	(.9)	(1.0)	(1.1)	[.001]	[.001]
Luck	1.0	1.1	1.1	1.89	...
	(.6)	(.5)	(1.1)	[N.S.]	

Note.—Standard deviations are given in parentheses and p levels in brackets. $df = 2,1317–1318$.

ability should also be more likely to believe that success can be obtained through diligent study. This proved to be the case. Correlations between the ratings made for these two statements were significant in all three cultures for both reading and mathematics. The respective correlations for statements referring to reading and to mathematics were .24 and .41 in Minneapolis, .42 and .40 in Taipei, and .38 and .59 in Sendai, all p's < .01.

Another approach to evaluating mothers' beliefs about the contribution

TABLE 17

Mother's Ratings of Their Agreement with Statements Related to Their Beliefs about Effort and Ability

	United States	Taiwan	Japan	F	Scheffé Contrasts
Same reading ability[a]	2.3	3.7	4.3	93.93	J > T > U
	(1.0)	(1.6)	(1.4)	[.001]	[.001] [.001]
Same math ability[b]	2.1	3.0	4.2	93.12	J > T > U
	(1.0)	(1.6)	(1.2)	[.001]	[.001] [.001]
Born with reading ability[c]	4.9	4.3	4.2	15.55	U > T & J
	(1.3)	(1.0)	(.9)	[.001]	[.001]
Born with math ability[d]	4.8	4.0	4.3	15.85	U > T & J
	(1.3)	(1.0)	(.9)	[.001]	[.001]
Good at reading[e]	3.7	5.2	5.2	52.22	T & J > U
	(1.5)	(1.6)	(1.0)	[.001]	[.001]
Good at math[f]	3.4	4.0	4.9	43.03	J > T > U
	(1.5)	(1.9)	(1.1)	[.001]	[.001] [.001]

Note.—$df = 2,382–385$.
[a] "People tend to have the same amount of reading ability" (1 = "strongly disagree," 7 = "strongly agree").
[b] "People tend to have the same amount of math ability" (1 = "strongly disagree," 7 = "strongly agree").
[c] "To what extent do you believe that ——— was born with his or her reading ability?" (1 = "very little," 7 = "a lot").
[d] "To what extent do you believe that ——— was born with his or her math ability?" (1 = "very little," 7 = "a lot").
[e] "Any student can be good at reading if he or she works hard enough" (1 = "strongly disagree," 7 = "strongly agree").
[f] "Any student can be good at math if he or she works hard enough" (1 = "strongly disagree," 7 = "strongly agree").

of ability to achievement is to examine their perceptions of their child's intellectual ability and academic potential. These two variables should be strongly related if mothers give greater emphasis to the role of ability in producing academic success than if mothers believe performance is strongly dependent on how hard the child works. In line with this prediction, the relation between the mothers' ratings of their child's intellectual ability described earlier and their ratings of their child's academic potential ("How well do you think ——— potentially could do in school?") was stronger in Minneapolis than in Taipei or Sendai; the correlations for mothers of first graders were, respectively, .66, .51, and .46 and for mothers of fifth graders .70, .44, and .36. The Minneapolis correlations differed significantly from those obtained for Taipei and Sendai, t's(435–450) = 2.38–5.11, p's < .05.

At another point in the follow-up interview, mothers were asked to rate the influence various factors can have on school performance. Included in this list were studying hard, intelligence, study habits, a good teacher, home environment, parental assistance, the curriculum, and luck. Ratings for the first two factors thus afford still another means of comparing the influence of effort (studying hard) and ability (innate intelligence) on academic achievement. Following the method used earlier, we subtracted the ratings for ability from those for effort. The difference was .2 for the American mothers, .8 for the Chinese mothers, and 1.0 for the Japanese mothers, $F(2,382) = 11.86, p < .001, J > U, p < .001, T > U, p < .01$.

The American mothers gave significantly lower ratings to effort than to study habits, a good teacher, home environment, and curriculum, t's(117) = 2.82–12.27, p's < .05 (see Fig. 6). The only factor that Chinese and Japanese mothers considered to be more important than effort was having a good teacher, t's(106,157) = 4.47, 3.97, p's < .001. The ratings given to effort departed significantly from all other ratings made by Taipei mothers, t's(104–106) = 2.79–16.69, all p's < .01, and, except for study habits and home environment, for the ratings made by Japanese mothers, t's(157) = 3.97–12.87, p's < .001.

Correlations were computed between mothers' ratings and their years of education to determine whether mothers with less education were as firm in their beliefs as were mothers with higher levels of education. The results are shown in Table 18. None of the relations was significant in Sendai, except for a tendency for better-educated mothers to give less emphasis to luck. In Taipei, the educational level of the mothers was positively related to studying hard, having a good teacher, and having a good home environment. The pattern for American mothers was quite different. Mothers with more years of schooling tended to give lower ratings to all variables other than intelligence and luck, where they gave higher ratings.

Mothers' prediction of test performance.—One consequence of a belief in the influence of innate ability is to believe it is possible to predict later

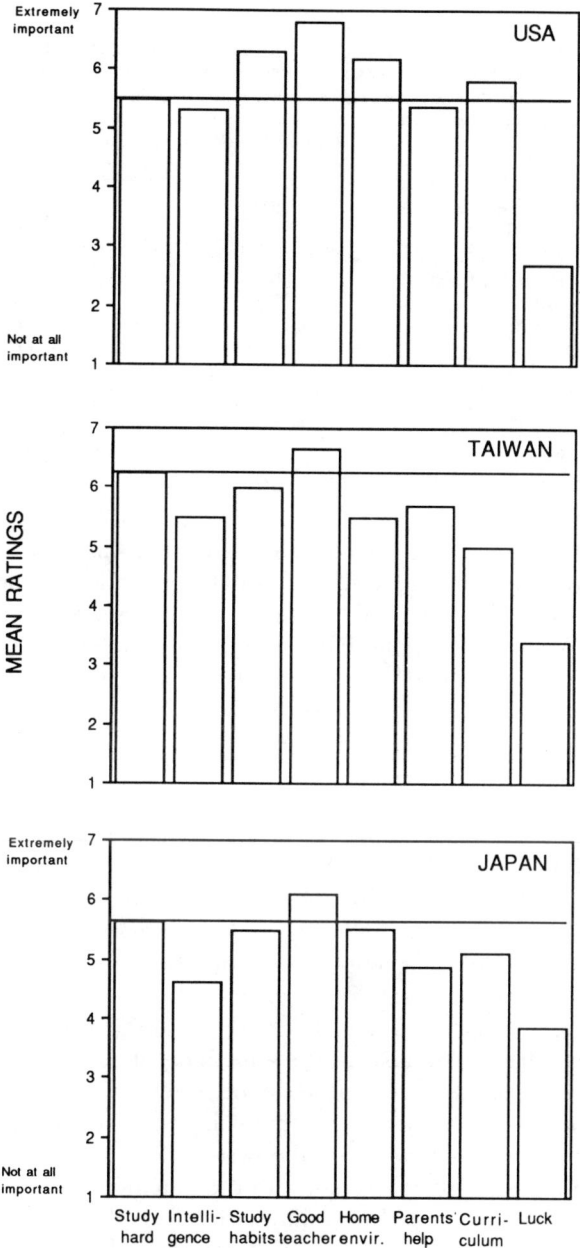

FIG. 6.—Mothers' ratings of the importance of eight factors related to school achievement. (Horizontal line represents rating for effort.)

TABLE 18

Correlations between Mother's Level of Education (Years of Schooling) and Her Ratings of the Importance of Various Factors Influencing School Performance

	United States	Taiwan	Japan
Study hard	−.06	.22*	.10
Intelligence	.29**	.15	.06
Study habits	−.20*	.08	.08
Good teacher	−.35***	.28**	.13
Home environment	−.20*	.23*	.05
Parental help	−.35***	.13	−.05
Curriculum	−.11	.06	.04
Luck	.18*	.01	−.17*

Note.—N's = 118–119 (United States); 106–109 (Taiwan); 157 (Japan).
* $p < .05$.
** $p < .01$.
*** $p < .001$.

performance at an early age. To test the possibility, American and Chinese mothers were asked the age at which they thought it is possible to predict how well a child will do on standard achievement tests given at the end of high school. More Minneapolis than Taipei mothers (38% vs. 10%) believed that such predictions could be made before the end of elementary school. (The question was not asked in Japan.)

CHILDREN'S BELIEFS

To what degree have elementary school children absorbed the beliefs about effort and ability held by adults in their culture? To answer this question, fifth graders in the follow-up study were asked to rate their agreement with a number of statements dealing with the role of effort, ability, and other factors in academic performance.

It is evident in Table 19 that children in all three cultures expressed a belief that children were able to do something about not doing well in reading or mathematics. However, while the American children showed the least agreement with the statements that children have the same ability in reading and mathematics and that the best student always works harder, they showed the greatest agreement with the statement that tests can show the child's natural ability. In these ratings, therefore, the American children were more likely than the Chinese or Japanese children to give greater emphasis to factors associated with innate ability. There was an apparent departure from this trend in the children's responses to the statement, "The best student in the class is always brighter than the other students." The

TABLE 19

MEAN RATINGS OF CHILDREN'S BELIEFS RELATED TO EFFORT AND ABILITY

	United States	Taiwan	Japan	F	Scheffé Contrasts
Not well in math[a]	2.5 (1.5)	2.2 (1.6)	2.6 (1.6)	3.86 [.05]	J > T [.05]
Not well in reading[b]	2.3 (1.4)	2.1 (1.6)	2.7 (1.7)	6.23 [.01]	J > T [.01]
Same math ability[c]	3.5 (1.5)	4.7 (1.9)	3.8 (1.4)	21.82 [.001]	T > U & J [.001]
Same reading ability[d]	3.4 (1.5)	4.7 (1.8)	3.9 (1.3)	26.42 [.001]	T > J > U [.001] [.05]
Works harder[e]	4.7 (1.8)	5.4 (1.7)	5.1 (1.6)	6.50 [.01]	T > U [.01]
Tests show[f]	4.7 (1.5)	3.9 (1.9)	2.8 (1.6)	45.43 [.001]	U > T > J [.001] [.001]
Brighter[g]	3.8 (1.6)	3.6 (1.8)	4.6 (1.5)	18.20 [.001]	J > U & T [.001]

NOTE.—Standard deviations are given in parentheses and p levels in brackets. df's = 2,442–444. Scales range from 1 ("strongly disagree") to 7 ("strongly agree").

[a] "If a person your age doesn't do well in math, there is probably nothing that person can do about it."
[b] "If a person your age doesn't do well in language arts, there is probably nothing that person can do about it."
[c] "Do you agree that everybody in your class has about the same amount of ability in math?"
[d] "Do you agree that everybody in your class has about the same amount of ability in language arts?"
[e] "The best student in the class always works harder than the other students."
[f] "The tests you take can show how much or how little natural ability you have."
[g] "The best student in the class is always brighter than the other students."

Chinese children showed the least agreement, but it was the Japanese rather than the American children who showed the strongest agreement.

Explanations of good and poor performance.—The influence of the outcome of a test on children's attributions was evaluated by telling the fifth graders in the follow-up study,

> Here is a list of reasons some students have given to explain why they have done well on a test. Think about a time you did well on a test or a time you did better than you usually do. Read each reason and then tell me how important it was for explaining why you did well on the test.

The reasons were related to ability ("because I am talented"), effort ("because I studied very hard before the test"), task difficulty ("because the test was very easy"), and luck ("because I was lucky"). Ratings were made on seven-point scales that ranged from 1 ("not an important reason") to 7 ("a very important reason").

The average difference between ratings for effort and ability were 1.8 (Chinese), 1.4 (American), and .8 (Japanese), $F(2,444) = 8.03, p < .001$, T > J, $p < .001$. When asked to imagine a time when they did not do well on a test, the average difference between ratings for effort and those for ability was again higher for Chinese (2.4) and American children (2.4) than for Japanese children (1.4), $F(2,443) = 9.63$, $p < .001$, $T > J$, $p < .001$, $U > J$, $p < .01$. The interpretation of these effects is difficult because there was a significant interaction between success-failure conditions and the children's level of achievement in both Minneapolis and Sendai, F's$(2,155,158) = 6.53$, 3.68, p's $< .05$. The American high achievers explained good performance by placing strong reliance on ability but considered their poor performance to be a result of lack of effort. Ratings by the Japanese children varied little according to their level of achievement, except for their greater reliance on lack of effort as an explanation of poor performance by high-achieving children. As for the Chinese children, the higher the level of achievement, the greater was their reliance on effort as an explanation of both good and bad performance.

CONCLUDING COMMENTS

Although more emphasis was generally given to effort than to ability as a basis for achievement, the relative strength of the belief in the importance of these factors differed among American, Chinese, and Japanese mothers. Relative to the Chinese and Japanese mothers, the American mothers placed greater emphasis on ability; Chinese and Japanese mothers placed greater emphasis on effort as an explanation for achievement.

When parents believe that success in school depends on ability in contrast to effort, they are less likely to foster participation in activities related to academic achievement that would elicit strong effort toward learning on the part of their children, such as doing homework, attending after-school classes, and receiving tutoring. American parents, in fact, did not use these activities with great frequency as means for improving their children's scholastic performance, even though they were willing to provide such supplemental activities for their children in sports, music, and art. Mothers who emphasize the importance of ability may ask if such activities are useful for children of low ability and may accept the poor performance of their children. If the child has high ability, the mother may question whether such activities are needed. A greater emphasis on ability appears to be related, therefore, to American children's lower accomplishments in elementary school.

Cultural beliefs were most strongly reflected in the responses of the Chinese and American children. As was the case with their mothers, Chinese children held strong beliefs about the importance of effort, and American children gave greater emphasis to the role of ability than did children in the other two cultures. The beliefs of Japanese children sometimes departed from those of their mothers; they emphasized the role of effort more strongly than the American children, but they also stressed the importance of ability.

It is difficult to account for the tendency of Japanese children to give relatively less emphasis to hard work than their mothers did. Perhaps the insistence of Japanese mothers on the utility of working hard leads Japanese children to ponder the complete validity of this dictum. After nearly 5 years of school, Japanese children may have found that it was not always the case that hard work resulted in scores as high as those of some other students. Their own experience may have offered them evidence that was counter to their mothers' persistent emphasis on hard work as the sufficient condition for success.

Whether differences in beliefs were responsible for the children's performance or whether the beliefs were a direct reflection of performance cannot be clearly determined. Children may work harder if they believe that achievement depends on effort, or they may believe that effort is important because they have been successful. Similarly, they may do better because they believe in their ability, or they may perceive themselves as able because of how well they have done. Each view may have special consequences for the child. Attributing success to high ability may lead to positive self-evaluations that carry over to new situations and enhance a child's confidence in attaining further success. Attributing poor performance to low ability may have devastating consequences. Once categorized and given a label as being a slow learner, it may be difficult for such children to accept the possibility of improvement. However, children who attribute their success to hard work may simply see themselves as hard workers and view each new situation as demanding renewed effort. In our view, the belief that increased effort pays off in improved performance is an important factor in accounting for the willingness of Chinese and Japanese children, teachers, and parents to spend so much time and effort on the children's academic work.

IX. MOTHERS' EVALUATIONS OF THEIR CHILD'S COGNITIVE ABILITIES, SCHOOL PERFORMANCE, MOTIVATION, AND PERSONALITY

To help us understand mothers' attitudes about their children's academic performance, we asked them to evaluate their children's cognitive abilities, academic achievement, and personality characteristics.

COGNITIVE ABILITIES

Mothers compared their child with other children of the same age in terms of ability to learn, remember, and express themselves verbally and in terms of their intellectual ability. The rating scale used in these comparisons had five defining statements ranging from "much below average" to "much above average," but mothers were allowed to use intermediate values, thus making nine points available for their ratings. Later in the interview, they also were asked to rate themselves on the same attributes according to how they remembered themselves in elementary school.

Had mothers displayed no bias in their ratings, the average rating for the representative sample of children from each city would have been "average." Instead, the average ratings depicted above-average children in all three cities, except for the Japanese mothers' ratings of the child's verbal expressiveness. American mothers gave their children the highest ratings, thereby displaying the strongest positive bias. Ratings made by Japanese mothers showed the least bias; their average ratings were nearest the "average" level. Ratings given by the Chinese mothers were between those made by the American and the Japanese mothers (see the left side of Fig. 7).

When the first graders had become fifth graders, the mothers rated the children on the same four characteristics. The results were consistent with those obtained earlier: the highest ratings were made by American mothers and the lowest by Japanese mothers. Ratings were relatively stable over the 4-year period. Correlations between ratings made for first and fifth graders were .39–.52 in Minneapolis, .36–.51 in Sendai, and .26–.33 in Taipei, all p's $< .01$.

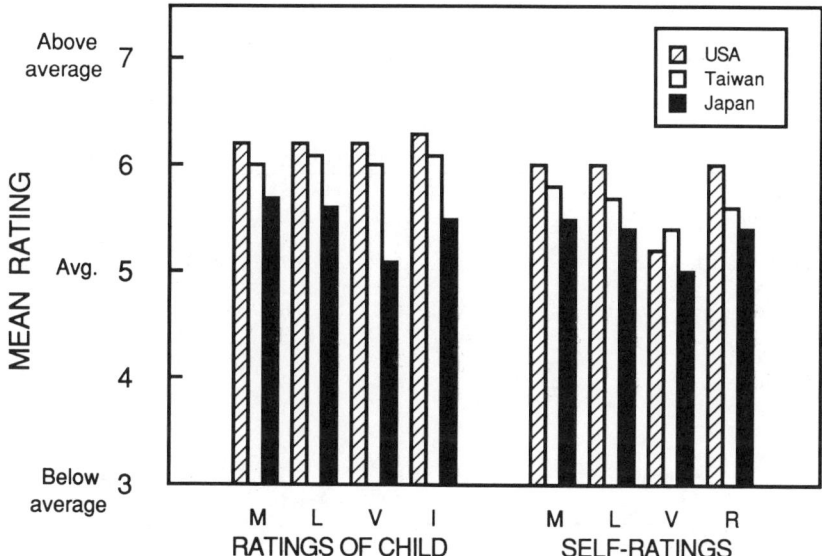

FIG. 7.—Mother's ratings of her child's and of her own cognitive abilities (M = memory; L = learning ability; V = verbal ability; I = intelligence; R = reasoning), F's$(2, 1291–1360) = 6.66–53.88$, p's $< .01$.

Results for mothers in the three cities fell into a pattern similar to that for ratings of the children (see the right side of Fig. 7). The mothers' average ratings reflected above-average self-evaluations in all cases, except for Japanese mothers' ratings of their verbal expressiveness. In other areas as well, Japanese mothers were the most modest, and American mothers tended to be the most confident. Reticence and modesty are characteristics commonly used to describe evaluations made by Japanese when referring to themselves (e.g., Christopher, 1983).

Mothers generally gave their child more favorable ratings than they gave themselves. They considered their child to be more able than they themselves were in learning, remembering, expressing themselves verbally, and in intelligence. All the differences between their ratings of themselves and of their child were statistically significant, t's$(396–476) = 2.25–8.91$, p's $< .05$, except for the Japanese mothers' ratings of verbal expression and intelligence, p's $> .05$.

Even though the mothers displayed different degrees of bias, mothers within each city appeared to be equally aware of their child's abilities in relation to those of other children. An overall index of the mothers' judgment of their child's cognitive abilities was obtained by averaging the four ratings; these scores were then correlated with the average scores the child obtained on the 10 cognitive tests that had been given at the same time the

MONOGRAPHS

TABLE 20

MOTHER'S RATINGS OF THEIR CHILD'S READING, MATHEMATICS, AND ACADEMIC PERFORMANCE

	United States	Taiwan	Japan	F	Scheffé Contrasts
Grade 1:					
Reading	6.0	5.8	5.3	10.28	U > J; T > J
	(1.7)	(1.7)	(1.4)	[.001]	[.001] [.05]
Mathematics	6.1	5.9	5.7	2.56	...
	(1.4)	(1.8)	(1.4)	[N.S.]	
Academic performance	6.2	6.1	5.6	12.00	U & T > J
	(1.3)	(1.6)	(1.2)	[.001]	[.001]
Grade 5:					
Reading	5.9	6.2	5.3	18.48	U > J; T > J
	(1.8)	(1.5)	(1.4)	[.001]	[.01] [.001]
Mathematics	5.9	5.5	5.6	3.18	U > T
	(1.6)	(1.8)	(1.5)	[.05]	[.05]
Academic performance	6.0	6.1	5.6	6.94	U > J; T > J
	(1.4)	(1.6)	(1.3)	[.01]	[.05] [.01]

NOTE.—Standard deviations are given in parentheses and p levels in brackets. df's = 2,677–678 (grade 1); 2,674–676 (grade 5). Scales range from 1 ("much below average") to 9 ("much above average").

mathematics test was administered. The r's obtained for first graders were .37 in Minneapolis, .50 in Taipei, and .41 in Sendai; for fifth graders they were, respectively, .55, .36, and .42, all p's < .001. Thus, mothers in all three locations had relatively accurate ideas about their children's abilities in relation to those of other children.

SCHOOL PERFORMANCE

Mothers also rated their child's general academic performance as well as his or her achievement in reading and mathematics. It is evident in Table 20 that the ratings were biased positively in all three cities. For example, less than 23% of any group of mothers rated their child as being below average in reading or mathematics.

The pattern of cultural differences we found for reading and mathematics achievement was not reflected in the average ratings made by mothers. American mothers gave their children high ratings in both subjects. Moreover, ratings given to American children for general academic performance were as high as those given by the Chinese mothers and were significantly higher than those made by the Japanese mothers.

Despite the positive biases about their child's level of achievement, mothers in each culture were aware of their child's relative standing in the group. All correlations between the mothers' ratings and the children's

TABLE 21

CORRELATIONS BETWEEN MOTHER'S RATINGS OF CHILD'S
ACHIEVEMENT AND CHILDREN'S ACHIEVEMENT SCORES

	United States	Taiwan	Japan
Grade 1:			
Mathematics	.55	.47	.48
Reading	.68	.46	.46
Grade 5:			
Mathematics	.50	.37	.54
Reading	.55	.29	.46

NOTE.—N's = 206–216 (United States); 224–236 (Taiwan); 237–239 (Japan); all p's < .001.

scores on the achievement tests in these two areas were significant. As can be seen in Table 21, however, the correlations related to reading were lower for mothers of fifth graders in Taipei than in Minneapolis, $t(424) = 3.38$, $p < .001$, and in Sendai, $t(457) = 2.23$, $p < .05$.

MOTIVATION

When asked about their child's motivation to do well in school, mothers in all three locations indicated motivational levels that were significantly above average. Again, American mothers generally gave the highest ratings (see Table 22). However, Chinese and Japanese mothers believed that their children's motivation to do well increased during the years of elementary school; American mothers did not. In the initial interviews, mothers gave the motivation of the Chinese and Japanese children higher ratings at fifth grade than at first grade, F's$(1456,473) = 3.86, 4.02$, p's < .05, but Ameri-

TABLE 22

MOTHER'S RATINGS OF THEIR CHILD'S MOTIVATION FOR ACHIEVEMENT

	United States	Taiwan	Japan	F	Scheffé Contrasts
Grade 1	6.4	5.9	5.5	18.56	U > T > J
	(1.5)	(1.6)	(1.3)	[.001]	[.01] [.05]
Grade 5	6.1	6.2	5.8	4.00	T > J
	(1.6)	(1.6)	(1.4)	[.05]	[.05]
Grade 5, follow-up[a]	6.7	6.7	6.0	6.80	U & T > J
	(2.0)	(1.8)	(1.5)	[.01]	[.05]

NOTE.—Standard deviations are given in parentheses and p levels in brackets. $df = 2,674$ (grade 1); 2,673 (grade 5); 2,380 (grade 5, follow-up). Scales range from 1 ("much below average") to 9 ("much above average").

[a] The seven-point scale was transformed into a nine-point scale here for purposes of comparison.

can mothers perceived their children as having lower motivation at the fifth grade than at the first, $F(1,418) = 4.65$, $p < .05$. These differences were partially replicated in the follow-up study. Chinese and Japanese mothers believed their child's motivation was significantly higher in the fifth grade than when they were in the first, t's$(102,157) = 2.97, 3.88$, p's $< .01$. There was no significant change between the first and the fifth grades in the ratings made by American mothers.

ACADEMIC POTENTIAL

The mothers' evaluations of their child's academic potential was gauged by asking them to predict how far their child would go in school. The majority of the American (65%), Chinese (71%), and Japanese (53%) mothers thought that their first grader would attain an undergraduate or a graduate degree; among mothers of fifth graders, the percentages declined somewhat, to 59% in Minneapolis, 63% in Taipei, and 50% in Sendai. In the follow-up study, many more of the American (84%) and Chinese mothers (84%) than of the Japanese mothers (57%) said that they would like to have their child attend college or graduate school. However, when asked whether they thought that this would be possible, more Minneapolis mothers (76%) than either Taipei or Sendai mothers (47% and 41%) responded in the affirmative. All these expectations were high, but those of the Sendai mothers were the most realistic. Currently, 44% of American youths attend college (U.S. Department of Education, 1988); the percentages are 43% in Taiwan (Ministry of Education, 1988) and 35% in Japan (Ministry of Education, Science, and Culture, 1978).

Mothers who believed that their child would attend college were asked why they thought he or she could go this far. The most common answers stressed either cognitive factors, such as having the necessary intelligence or ability, or motivational factors, such as studying hard, having ambition, and being task oriented. The American mothers were more likely to mention cognitive than motivational factors (27% vs. 18%), the Chinese mothers mentioned each with equal frequency (23%), and the Japanese mothers more often referred to motivational rather than cognitive factors (30% vs. 11%). These different emphases are similar to the findings discussed earlier concerning ability and effort.

In a final question related to academic abilities, mothers were asked to indicate on a nine-point scale how well they thought their child "potentially could do in school." Only 7% of the Minneapolis mothers and 13% of the Sendai mothers rated their child's academic potential as average or below. Among Taipei mothers, however, 41% made such ratings—a more accurate evaluation of potential academic accomplishment of a representative sample of children.

The mothers' ratings revealed a discrepancy between their perceptions of their child's potential and his or her academic performance. The mean difference between their two ratings was 1.34 in Sendai, 1.02 in Minneapolis, and .20 in Taipei, $F(2,1346) = 110.41, p < .001, J > U > T, p$'s $< .001$. Thus, the Chinese mothers believed that their children were working up to their potential to a greater degree than did the Japanese and American mothers. The Japanese mothers obviously held very high standards for their children. Even though Japanese children were doing well in school, their mothers thought that they could do even better.

PERSONALITY CHARACTERISTICS

Mothers were asked to rate some personality characteristics that described their child "the way he or she is at home." Mothers rated these characteristics on five-point scales, with values ranging from "almost never like that" to "almost always like that."

The ratings yielded a favorable picture, especially of American children (see Table 23). Among the three groups of mothers, American mothers saw their children as being the most self-confident, sociable, curious, creative, persistent, and obedient. They saw them as seldom shy and restless but as seeking approval. Ratings given by Japanese mothers described children who were the least likely to show self-confidence, obedience, and approval seeking and the most likely to be shy and anxious. Chinese mothers found their children to be the least often curious, creative, and persistent. Chinese children were rated as the most restless but the least anxious of the three cultural groups.

RESPONSIBILITY IN DAILY LIFE

The stereotyped image of the American is that of a ruggedly independent individual. This image, as applied to children, was not supported in our interview with mothers. Mothers were told that "there are many daily activities in a family where someone has to make decisions or take responsibility" and were asked to decide the degree to which it was the parents' or the child's responsibility in making decisions in seven areas of children's daily life. Except for the choice of clothes, American mothers did not assign more responsibility to their children than did Chinese and Japanese mothers (see Fig. 8). It was typically the Japanese mother who believed that

TABLE 23
Mother's Ratings of Child's Personality Characteristics

	United States	Taiwan	Japan	F	Scheffé Contrasts
Self-confidence	3.8	3.4	3.1	69.89	U > T > J
	(.8)	(1.0)	(1.0)	[.001]	[.001] [.001]
Sociability	4.3	4.1	4.2	10.59	U > T; U > J
	(.7)	(.7)	(1.0)	[.001]	[.001] [.01]
Curiosity	4.1	3.5	3.8	58.15	U > J > T
	(.7)	(.9)	(1.0)	[.001]	[.001] [.001]
Creativity	4.0	3.1	3.5	98.88	U > J > T
	(.8)	(1.0)	(1.1)	[.001]	[.001] [.001]
Persistence	3.8	3.0	3.3	66.36	U > J > T
	(.9)	(1.1)	(1.1)	[.001]	[.001] [.001]
Seeking approval	4.1	3.8	3.6	35.80	U > T > J
	(.8)	(.9)	(1.0)	[.001]	[.001] [.001]
Obedience	3.9	3.8	3.5	25.37	U > T > J
	(.7)	(.9)	(1.1)	[.001]	[.05] [.001]
Anxiety	2.6	2.2	3.0	81.10	J > U > T
	(1.0)	(.9)	(1.1)	[.001]	[.001] [.001]
Restlessness	2.6	3.1	2.8	25.05	T > U & J
	(1.1)	(1.2)	(1.2)	[.001]	[.001]
Shyness	2.5	2.7	2.8	4.75	J > U
	(1.1)	(1.2)	(1.3)	[.01]	[.01]

Note.—Standard deviations are given in parentheses and p levels in brackets. df's = 2,1315–1358. Scales ranged from 1 ("almost never") to 5 ("almost always").

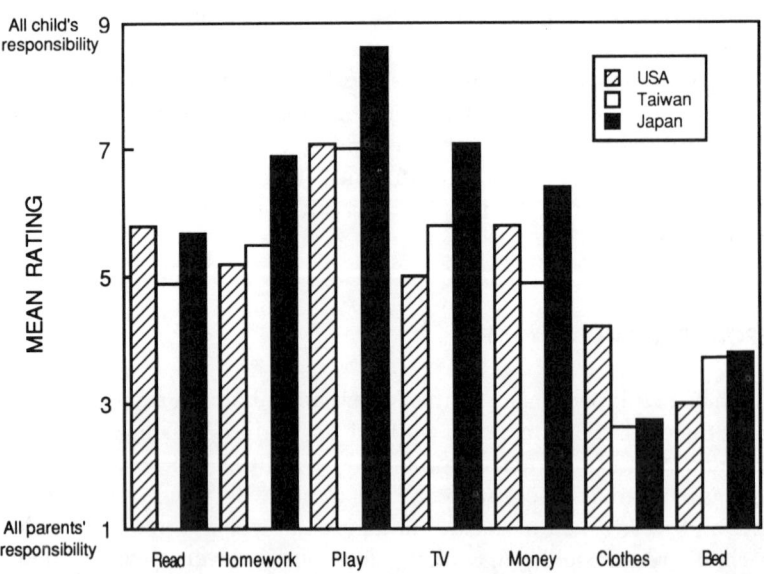

FIG. 8.—Mother's ratings of child's and parents' degree of responsibility for various activities, including choosing child's reading material; choosing which television programs child may watch; deciding how child can spend his or her money; choosing child's playmates; deciding child's bedtime; deciding clothes to purchase for child; making sure child's homework is completed, F's(2,1345–1360) = 13.43–108.07, p's < .001.

the child should be given responsibility; this was the case for choice of playmates, television programs, spending money, and getting homework done. The importance in Japanese culture of establishing a strong sense of self-responsibility in children is evident in contexts other than the home. Lewis (1984), in her description of techniques used by kindergarten teachers, gives many vivid examples of how they promote responsibility among children.

CONCLUDING COMMENTS

The popular image of the Asian mother was not upheld. Chinese and Japanese mothers did not appear to be excessively demanding persons who held unrealistic aspirations for their children. Mothers in all three cultures demonstrated sensitivity to their child's standing in relation to his or her peers, but the average ratings differed greatly among the three cultures. When mothers are as positive as American mothers seem to be about their child's current academic performance and cognitive abilities, they may provide little incentive for their children to strive for higher levels of achievement. Indeed, the stronger motivation to do well in school that appeared in the ratings of the fifth-grade compared to the first-grade Chinese and Japanese children was not found for American children. In general, it was the Japanese mothers who displayed the most realistic appraisal of their children's abilities and accomplishments and who showed the greatest willingness to grant their children independence in undertaking routine activities in their daily lives.

X. MOTHERS' SATISFACTION WITH THEIR CHILD'S SCHOOL PERFORMANCE AND EVALUATIONS OF CURRICULUM AND SCHOOL

SATISFACTION WITH ACADEMIC PERFORMANCE

We asked mothers how satisfied they were with their child's current academic performance. Nearly all American mothers were "satisfied" or "very satisfied"—frequencies in strong contrast with those of the Chinese and Japanese mothers (see the top of Fig. 9).

Cross-national differences were even more dramatic when only the "very satisfied" mothers are considered. Less than 5% of the Chinese and Japanese mothers but over 40% of the American mothers said that they were very satisfied with their child's performance. This trend continued 4 years later in the follow-up interview (see Fig. 9). It is also evident that the Chinese and Japanese mothers were more likely than American mothers to adopt successively higher criteria for their children's academic performance as their children became older. Chinese and Japanese mothers were less satisfied with the performance of their fifth graders than of their first graders. The longitudinal data between the first and the fifth grades also revealed greater declines in the satisfaction expressed by mothers in Taipei and Sendai than by mothers in Minneapolis.

As would be expected, mothers of children who received higher scores in reading and mathematics were more satisfied than were mothers whose children received lower scores. This is depicted in Figure 10. Mean z scores derived from the overall achievement scores are plotted in Figure 10 as a function of the satisfaction within each country expressed by the mothers.

Comparisons of the scores of fifth graders with those they obtained when they were in the first grade indicate that American mothers tended to relax their standards over the 4 years whereas Chinese and Japanese mothers tended to make them more severe. The basis of this statement is apparent when the data in the top of Figure 10 are compared with those in the bottom. In Taipei and Sendai, maternal criteria for dissatisfaction appear to have been similar at both grades, but the criteria for Minneapolis mothers appear to have been less stringent at the fifth than at the first grade.

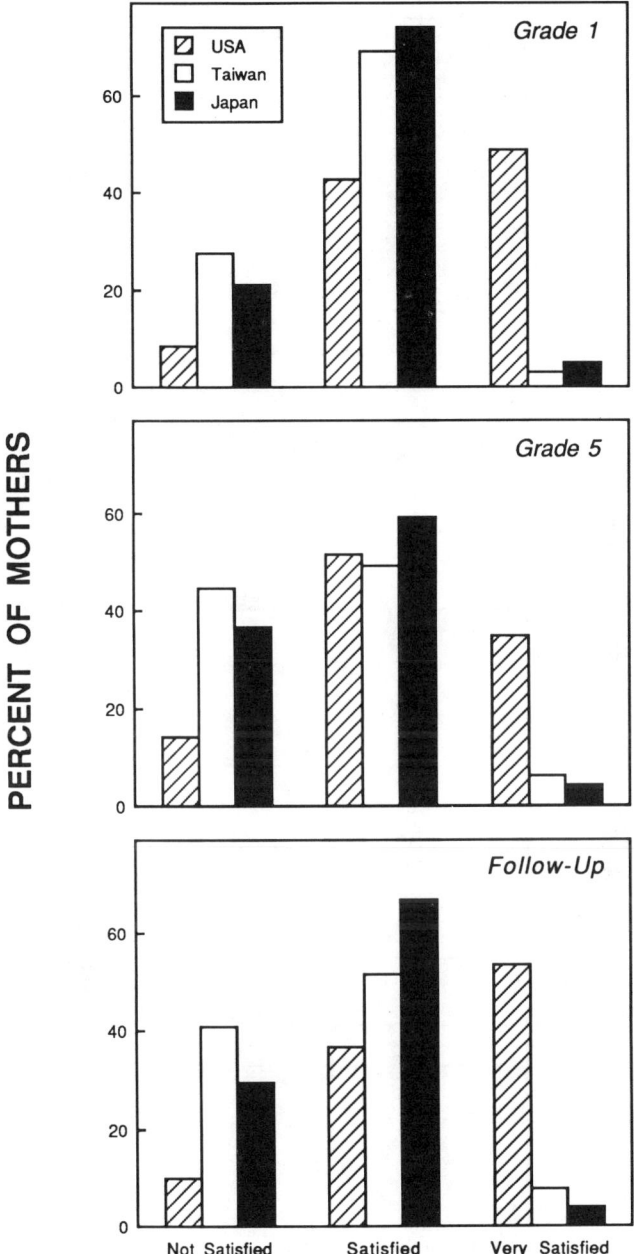

FIG. 9.—Mothers' degree of satisfaction with their child's schoolwork

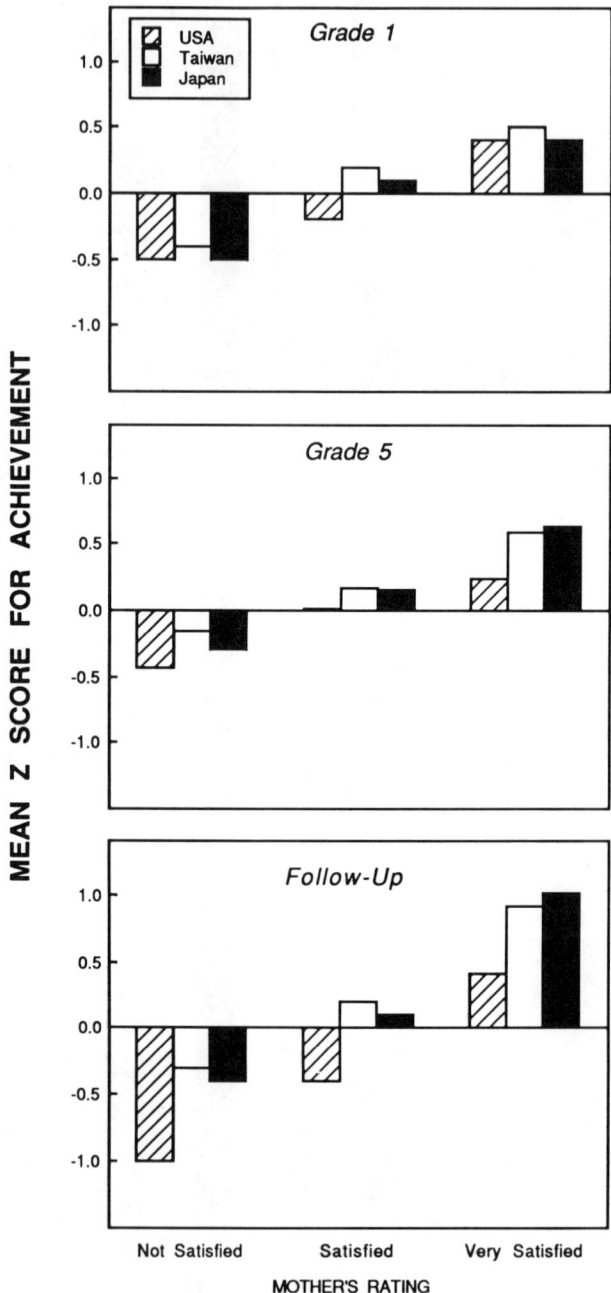

Fig. 10.—z scores of child's achievement according to mother's level of satisfaction

Differences among cities were not significant at the first grade, $p > .05$, but were significant in the follow-up study when those children were in the fifth grade, $F(2,96) = 3.49$, $p < .05$. A different trend appeared for children whose mothers indicated that they were "very satisfied" with their child's level of achievement. In this case, Chinese and Japanese mothers appear to have adopted higher criteria at the fifth grade than at the first, while the criteria of the American mothers were unchanged. As was the case with the scores for mothers who were not satisfied, differences among cities were not significant at the first grade, $p > .05$, but were significant 4 years later at the fifth grade, $F(2,73) = 5.90$, $p < .01$. Values for mothers of fifth graders in the initial study followed the same trends as those for mothers in the follow-up study but did not differ significantly among the three cities.

Another indication of lower standards on the part of the American mothers appears in scores of children whose mothers said that they were "satisfied" with their child's performance. Having their child near the mean was sufficient for the American mothers to be satisfied; having a child above the mean was more often a requirement for mothers in Taipei and Sendai.

Within each city, mothers who believed more strongly that their child was performing up to potential were more satisfied with their child's performance. Correlations between the mothers' ratings made in response to the question, "How well do you think ——— potentially *could* do in school," and their ratings of their satisfaction with their child's current academic performance were consistently significant in each city and at each grade, r's $= .22-.55$, p's $< .001$.

Mothers in the three cultures relied on different criteria for judging their child's academic performance. Three alternatives were suggested to the mothers: comparisons with other children, effort, and grades. American and Japanese mothers based their judgments primarily on how hard their child tried: 72% of the American and 65% of the Japanese mothers ranked this as their first consideration. Grades were the most important index of success for Chinese mothers; the majority (54%) indicated that the primary basis of judgment was how far the child was from a perfect score.

EFFECTIVENESS OF SCHOOL

Not only were the American mothers more positive than Chinese and Japanese mothers about their child's performance, but they were also satisfied with the job the schools were doing in educating their child. In the initial study, the majority (91%) of the Minneapolis mothers rated the school as doing an "excellent" or "good" job of educating their child, but only 41% of the Taipei mothers and 39% of the Sendai mothers made such judgments. There were no significant differences between the responses of mothers of the first and fifth graders. Similar results were found in the follow-up study; 81% of the American mothers, 40% of the Chinese mothers, and 37% of the Japanese mothers gave their child's school ratings of "excellent" or "good."

CHANGES IN MOTHERS' PERCEPTIONS OF THEIR CHILD'S PERFORMANCE

In the follow-up study, mothers of fifth graders were asked to compare their child's current performance with that in the first grade. More than half the mothers thought that their child's level of performance had changed. In Minneapolis, they were far more likely to think that the change had led to improvement (48%) than to decline (8%), but in Taipei they were more likely to believe that their child's performance had declined (40%) than that it had improved (22%). The pattern in Sendai was similar to that in Minneapolis; 41% reported improvement and 15% decline. The most common explanations of why there had been a change made by the Chinese (40%) and the Japanese (27%) mothers were related to improved study habits, such as working harder, possessing better study skills, or the child applying himself or herself more effectively. Few American mothers (9%) gave this type of reason. The prevalence of other explanations of their child's improvement differed less markedly among the three groups of mothers. A belief that their child had a better teacher was mentioned by 21%, 12%, and 19% of mothers in Minneapolis, Taipei, and Sendai and a belief that their child had developed more positive personality characteristics, such as increased maturity, greater independence, and greater self-confidence, by 20%, 16%, and 12%, respectively. However, the Chinese parents were less likely than the American and Japanese parents to attribute the improvement to their child's having a more positive attitude about school and learning. This response was made by only 4% of the Taipei mothers but by 20% of the Minneapolis and 28% of the Sendai mothers.

When asked to explain the *decline* in their child's performance, the Chinese and Japanese mothers attributed it primarily to worse study habits (27% and 31%, respectively) or to the greater difficulty of the material presented in school (35% and 27%). So few of the American mothers believed that their child's performance had declined that a breakdown of their explanations was not attempted.

Mothers' judgments of whether there had been improvement, decline, or no change in their child's academic performance between the initial and the follow-up study were unrelated to the actual change in children's performance between these two periods in either Minneapolis or Taipei (i.e., there were no significant differences in children's summary achievement scores according to the mothers' judgments). In Sendai, mothers were more aware of a change in their child's performance; children whose mothers reported improvement had a positive average change in z scores (.18); those mothers who reported a decline had a negative average change in z scores $(-.12)$, $F(2,154) = 4.89$, $p < .01$.

DIFFICULTY OF CURRICULUM

In all three locations, over 80% of the mothers at both grades considered the level of difficulty of the curriculum to be "about right." Only 2% in Minneapolis, 14% in Taipei, and 13% in Sendai believed that the curriculum was too difficult. Mothers who thought that the curriculum was too easy were somewhat more numerous in Minneapolis (10%) than in either Taipei (3%) or Sendai (2%). There was little change in the opinions of the American mothers during the subsequent 4 years, but 28% of the Chinese mothers and 30% of the Japanese mothers thought that the curriculum had become too hard.

CONCLUDING COMMENTS

Minneapolis mothers were positive and enthusiastic about their child's education. Those in Taipei and Sendai were much more critical. Although it would be easy to conclude that the American mothers were inattentive to their children's academic progress and were less able to evaluate the status of their children in relation to other children, they were no less accurate than the others in the match between their judgments and their child's level of achievement. We believe that the difference between the attitudes of American and Asian mothers stemmed from the lower academic standards of the American mothers than those held by the Chinese and Japanese mothers. Moreover, American mothers had lower standards for fifth graders than for first graders. American mothers were less critical, and they therefore expected less of their children and of the schools.

Why should American mothers express such high levels of satisfaction with their child's performance? One likely explanation lies in the lack of a standard to which they can refer. There is no national or state curriculum that defines what children should learn at each grade in school, and few mothers have information about how other children are performing. Without such referents, it is difficult to assess the adequacy of a child's performance. Another possible explanation is the American mothers' lower emphasis on academic achievement. It is much easier to be satisfied with moderate levels of performance when it is not deemed to be of critical importance to a child's future.

The satisfaction of American parents is not restricted to Minneapolis. In our current research, similarly high degrees of satisfaction with their children's academic performance and with the job that schools are doing in educating their children were expressed by mothers in the Chicago metropolitan area (Stevenson et al., in press).

These data pose an interesting dilemma. American mothers, whose children had average achievement scores below those of the Chinese and Japanese children, were the most positive about the schools and how their children were performing. With such high levels of positive response, it is difficult to suggest how innovations in educational practice could begin. The optimistic approval expressed by American mothers conveyed no sense of urgency about improving the educational programs in elementary schools. Unless a need for improvement is expressed, change is unlikely to occur.

XI. PROBLEMS IN SCHOOLING ACCORDING TO MOTHERS AND TEACHERS

During a child's 6 years of elementary school, parents and teachers must respond to children's academic problems. Our purpose in this section is to explore the perceptions of parents and teachers about these problems and how they might be alleviated.

PROBLEMS IN READING AND MATHEMATICS

When asked if their first graders had displayed problems in reading, 26% of the American mothers, 44% of the Chinese mothers, and 19% of the Japanese mothers responded in the affirmative. For the children in the fifth grade, these percentages were 34%, 27%, and 18%. The high percentage of problems noted among Chinese first graders is probably a function of having to learn a large number of Chinese characters during the beginning stages of reading

In response to a parallel question about mathematics, more of the Chinese than of the American or Japanese mothers reported that their child had encountered a problem. In the first grade, the percentages were 10% (Minneapolis), 33% (Taipei), and 15% (Sendai), and for fifth graders they had increased to 28%, 68%, and 30%, respectively.

These data indicate that mothers of fifth graders in Minneapolis believed that their child had somewhat more problems in reading than in mathematics (34% vs. 28%), whereas the converse—more problems in mathematics than in reading—was reported in Taipei (68% vs. 27%) and Sendai (30% vs. 18%). These data parallel maternal beliefs concerning the two subjects. More Taipei (83%) and Sendai (82%) than Minneapolis (47%) mothers thought that mathematics was more difficult, but 43% of the Minneapolis and less than 15% of the Taipei and Sendai mothers thought that reading was more difficult. Small percentages of the mothers thought that the two subjects were equally difficult: 1% (Minneapolis), 13% (Taipei), and 4% (Sendai).

Mothers were reasonably effective in judging the presence or absence of a problem. Children who were judged by their mothers to have a problem also obtained lower scores in the given subject. The differences for both subjects were significant for the American and Japanese children at both the first and the fifth grades, F's(1199–235) = 7.78–36.94, p's < .01, and for the Chinese children for first-grade mathematics and fifth-grade reading, F's(1,221,233) = 8.35, 22.01, p's < .01.

When problems were encountered, how were they solved? For first and fifth graders with reading problems, over half (55%) the responses of the American mothers, 72% of those of Chinese mothers, and 75% of those of Japanese mothers indicated that they depended on the family for helping their child. Few of the responses concerned looking to the school as a source of help for reading problems: 18% of the responses of American mothers and only 1% of the responses of Chinese and Japanese mothers. Mothers' responses to their child's problems in mathematics were very similar to those in reading. Most responses—from 80% to 83%—indicated that assistance to the child came from within the family.

Despite the fact that communication between parents and teachers is frequent in Taipei and Sendai, parents generally did not seek frequent personal interaction with their children's teachers. Teachers reported that, on the average, during the previous month they had been asked to talk about an individual child by two parents in Sendai and Minneapolis and five parents in Taipei. (It should be kept in mind in comparing these numbers that Sendai and Taipei classrooms contained many more children than the Minneapolis classrooms.) Mothers also reported little direct interaction. The mothers estimated that they or their husband had spoken during the school year individually with their child's teacher—not necessarily about a problem—an average of five times in Minneapolis, four times in Taipei, and twice in Sendai. When individual conferences were requested, the major topics were the expected ones: academic achievement, scholastic progress, and social and behavioral problems.

COPING WITH A BAD TEACHER

We asked mothers what they would do if they found that their child's teacher was not doing a good job with their child. Their responses were very different in the three cities (see Fig. 11). Minneapolis mothers most frequently replied that they would contact the teacher and administrators at the school or try to have the child transferred to another teacher or school. Taipei mothers said that they would seek help within the family or contact the child's teacher. The predominant response of Japanese mothers (69%) was to do nothing. In terms of the Japanese school system, this response was

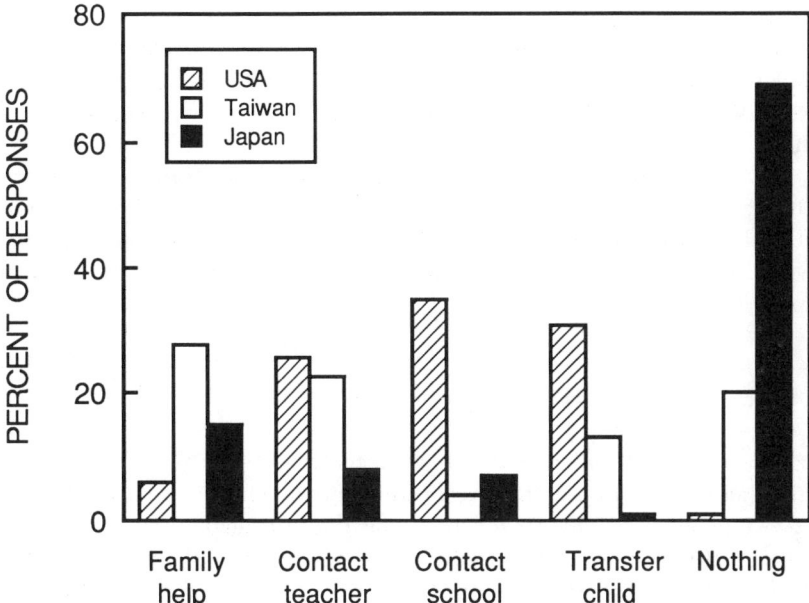

Fig. 11.—Percentages of mothers' responses suggesting different ways for coping with a bad teacher.

more realistic than it may first appear. Educational policies in Japan are firm, and parents have little hope of being able to change their child's classroom or school.

TYPES OF PARENTAL ASSISTANCE

Mothers were most likely to suggest greater parent-child interaction when they were asked how they thought they could best help their children do well in school. This was the case for 75% of the responses made in Minneapolis, 67% in Taipei, and 47% in Sendai. Fewer mothers (less than 10% in each city) suggested actions involving the child's teacher or the school. Over one-third of the Japanese mothers (34%) but few Chinese and American mothers (8% and 6%) referred to a good study environment in terms of providing good reading and reference materials, exposing the child to cultural and social activities, being a good model, and having the child get proper food, rest, and exercise. A few mothers, mostly in Sendai, suggested simply accepting the child's performance.

Responses in the category of parent-child interaction were broken down into the subcategories of help (help with or supervise homework, read to the child, participate in learning experiences with the child), encouragement (encourage and support the child, express positive feelings about the child, be patient or understanding), and involvement (interact or communicate with the child, talk about school, be more aware of what is going on at school).

Of these, help was mentioned by about 35% of the mothers in all three cultures. The proportion mentioning encouragement was smaller in Sendai (11%) than in Minneapolis (56%) or Taipei (47%). Greater involvement was favored more by the American mothers (43%) than by the Chinese (6%) or Japanese (4%) mothers.

SOURCES OF HELP WITH SCHOOLWORK

In Taipei, 96% of the mothers reported that their child received help with schoolwork at home; the proportions were much lower in Sendai (62%) and Minneapolis (67%). In terms of the time devoted to such help, the mothers' estimates in the three cities were, respectively, 27, 29, and 20 min per day. These estimates were unrelated to maternal employment status in any of the cities, r's = $-.13$–$.08$, p's > $.05$, but there were some significant associations between children's level of achievement and the amount of help that they received at home. Greater amounts of help tended to be provided to low achievers in Sendai and Minneapolis, r's = $-.21$ and $-.25$, p's < $.01$, for the Japanese first and fifth graders, $r = -.22$, $p < .01$, for the American fifth graders. This was not the case with the Chinese children, r's = $-.05$ and $.04$, p's > $.05$.

According to the mothers' reports, help with children's schoolwork in Minneapolis and Sendai came mainly from the mothers. Over 60% of the mothers but few fathers (less than 10%) were reported to be primarily responsible for assisting the child with reading; however, more fathers (about 30%) did so in the case of mathematics. In Taipei families, assistance was reported to be distributed more broadly among family members; between 20% and 40% of the mothers, fathers, and older siblings were mentioned as providing help in both reading and mathematics.

The relative importance of the mother and father in assisting their children was assessed by asking mothers whether the mother, the father, or the teacher was the most important source of help. After determining the rank order, the interviewer asked how many points the mother would give to the person ranked second and to the person ranked first if she had nine points to apportion between the first and second ranks (one point was given to the person ranked lowest).

Teachers were assigned the largest number of points in all three cities (means of 5.9, 6.0, and 6.1 in Minneapolis, Taipei, and Sendai), and in all three cities the means for the mother exceeded those for the father (2.6 vs. 2.0; 2.2 vs. 1.7; and 2.2 vs. 1.7 in the three respective cities). Minneapolis mothers assigned significantly more points to the role of the mothers and fathers than did mothers in the other two cities, F's$(2,1325) = 17.79, 11.28$, p's $< .001$, U $>$ T and J, p's $< .01$, but mothers in Taipei and Sendai assigned significantly more points to the teachers than did the Minneapolis mothers, $F(2,1326) = 23.68, p < .001$, T and J $>$ U, p's $< .001$.

SUGGESTED CHANGES IN EMPHASIS IN SCHOOLS

Despite their reported satisfaction with their children's schools (cf. Chap. X), more Minneapolis than Taipei or Sendai mothers made suggestions about possible changes in what schools emphasize. Across both grades of the initial study, such suggestions were made by 44%, 34%, and 27% of the Minneapolis, Taipei, and Sendai mothers. Four years later in the follow-up study, the percentages were even greater: 61%, 47%, and 54%, respectively.

Areas viewed as requiring greater emphasis.—Suggestions of factors needing greater emphasis were categorized into five types: academic subjects; nonacademic subjects (e.g., gym, music), training in social skills and moral education, school environment (e.g., smaller classes, more individualized instruction, improved physical facilities), and teacher's behavior (e.g., more discipline, greater sensitivity to individual differences, higher motivation, better communication with parents). The percentages of responses in each area are given in Figure 12.

Minneapolis mothers who made suggestions about improving education were most likely to mention academic areas; mention of nonacademic activities and of social and moral training were most frequent in Taipei; and, except for nonacademic activities, the percentage of responses in the other categories was about equal in Sendai.

The six academic and nonacademic subjects included in the mothers' comments were reading, math, science, "basics," music and art, and gym. The percentages of responses in which each was mentioned are shown in Figure 13. Reading was mentioned most frequently by the Minneapolis and Sendai mothers. In Taipei, where children received the highest scores, it was seldom mentioned. Academic subjects were already getting sufficient attention in the opinion of Taipei mothers; they most frequently mentioned music, art, or gym. Mathematics and science were infrequently mentioned as subjects needing more emphasis in any of the cities.

Among mothers who referred to teachers' behavior, few had specific criticisms, except for the wish for more opportunity for individualized instruction. Over a third of the Minneapolis mothers (36%), 48% of the Sendai

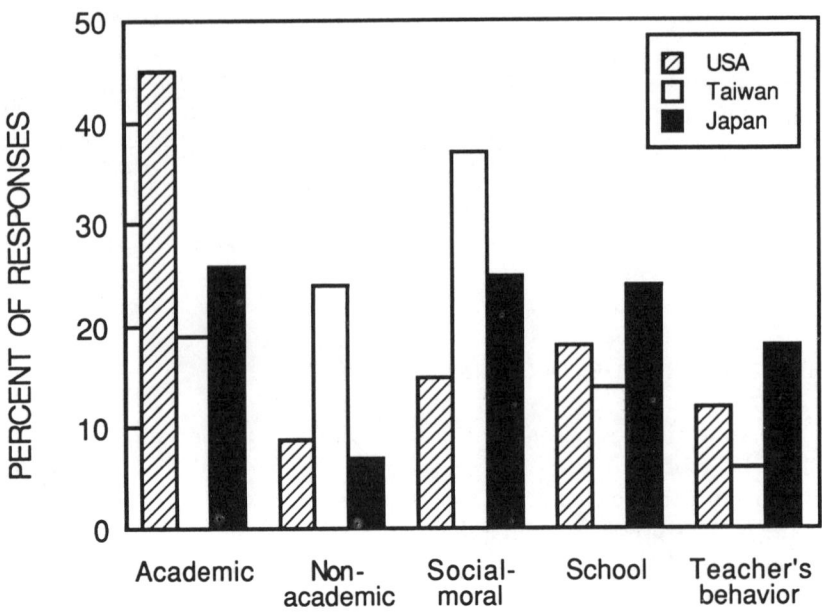

FIG. 12.—Percentage of mothers' suggestions concerning areas needing more emphasis in school.

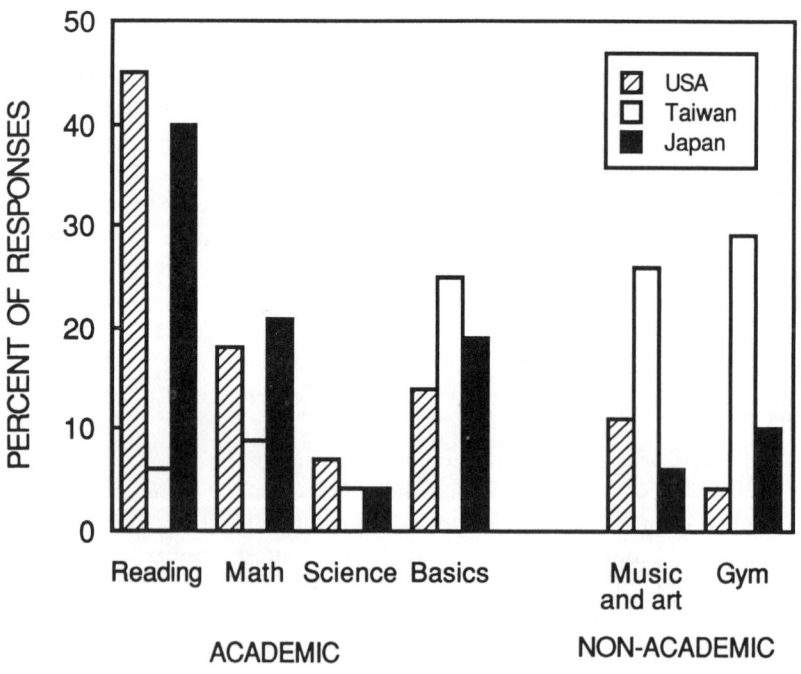

FIG. 13.—Percentage of mothers' suggestions concerning academic and nonacademic areas needing more emphasis in school.

mothers, and 27% of the Taipei mothers who suggested that some aspects of schools were underemphasized mentioned the need for individualized instruction. Fewer than 6% of all mothers across the three cities mentioned other areas of possible improvement on the part of the teachers, such as their motivation, emphasis on creativity, and communication with parents.

TEACHERS' PROBLEMS

Among the 40 teachers in each of the three cities, the difficulty most frequently mentioned by those in Minneapolis (23) and Sendai (20) was meeting the demands on their time, both inside and outside their classrooms. In Taipei, this problem was mentioned by only six teachers.

The problem of motivating children and of maintaining control of the classroom and children's attention were mentioned by 14 Minneapolis teachers but by fewer than four teachers in Taipei or Sendai. The only other categories mentioned by more than a few Chinese (eight) and Japanese (one) teachers were meeting individual needs of children in the classroom and resolving conflicts between the parents' wishes and their own goals. It is understandable that teachers should have difficulties in meeting the individual needs of children when there are 40 or 50 children in the classroom, but 14 American teachers also mentioned this problem, even though there were never as many as 30 children in their classrooms.

WHAT TEACHERS BELIEVE IS IMPORTANT FOR ACADEMIC PROGRESS

Teachers' views about the usefulness of various activities for children's academic development were obtained by asking them to rate each of 16 activities on a nine-point scale ranging from "not useful" to "very useful." Remarkable similarity in the rank ordering of these activities emerged in the three cities (see Table 24). Friendly relations with the children, verbal praise, and individual instruction received the highest ranks. Physical punishment received the lowest. There were several surprises. First, drill received a high rank by all three groups of teachers, but memorization, a closely related activity, was considered more important by the Taipei than by the Minneapolis or Sendai teachers. In fact, Chinese elementary school teachers often require their pupils to memorize long narratives and even long sections of their reading textbooks. Second, teachers in Minneapolis placed greater importance on strict discipline and recitation than did teachers in Taipei or Sendai. Third, among other activities in which there was great disagreement were nonverbal rewards, which were considered more important by the Chinese teachers; study groups, which were considered less

TABLE 24

TEACHER'S RATINGS OF USEFULNESS OF THE FOLLOWING ITEMS FOR CHILDREN'S ACADEMIC ACHIEVEMENT

	UNITED STATES		TAIWAN		JAPAN	
	Rank	Mean	Rank	Mean	Rank	Mean
Friendly relations between teacher and pupil	1	8.6	2	8.4	3	7.6
Use of verbal or written praise	1	8.6	3	8.2	2	7.7
Teacher's rapport with child's family	3	8.2	5	7.8	6	7.1
Individual instruction	4	8.0	1	8.6	1	8.2
Drills	5	7.1	5	7.8	5	7.3
Nonverbal reward	6	6.8	4	8.0	9	6.0
Strict discipline	7	6.7	12	7.0	13	5.3
Study groups	8	6.5	15	6.3	8	6.4
Recitation	9	6.4	14	6.8	14	5.4
Quizzes	10	6.2	9	7.4	7	6.9
Exams	11	6.0	8	7.5	10	5.9
Teacher available after class	12	5.9	7	7.6	4	7.4
Extracurricular	13	5.8	12	7.0	12	5.5
Memorization	14	5.2	11	7.2	15	5.1
Homework	15	4.4	10	7.3	11	5.8
Physical punishment	16	1.9	16	5.4	16	4.2

NOTE.—Ranks are based on the mean ratings made by the teachers on a nine-point scale ranging from 1 ("not useful") to 9 ("very useful").

important by the Chinese teachers; and teacher availability, which was considered more important by Chinese and Japanese than by American teachers. Fourth, American teachers considered homework inferior only to physical punishment in its usefulness to their pupils' academic achievement. Chinese and Japanese teachers were much more positive about homework. The average rating by the Chinese teachers was 7.3 and by the Japanese teachers 5.8. American teachers gave homework a rating of 4.4—a value below the midpoint of the scale.

IMPROVING TEACHING CONDITIONS

To assess teachers' perceptions of the current situation in their school, we asked them to assume that it had been given a large amount of extra money to be spent during one school year and that they were to recommend ways that the money should be spent. Their answers were categorized into five areas: reduce class size, improve academic programs, purchase academic equipment, educational activities, and nonacademic activities (e.g., art supplies, after-school sports, traffic safety, lunch, and gym). The categories mentioned most frequently by Taipei and Sendai teachers were for new academic equipment for the school and for nonacademic activities (see the top panel of Fig. 14). Despite the large size of the classes in Taipei and Sendai elementary schools, no teacher suggested that the funds be used to

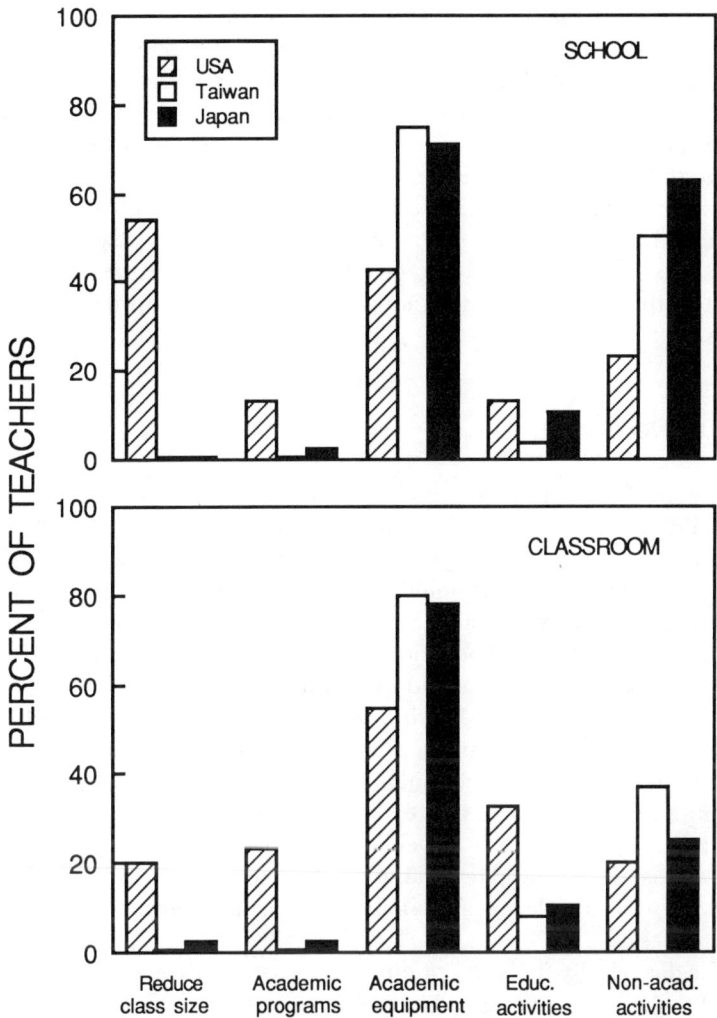

FIG. 14.—Percentages of teachers who suggested various changes within the school and within the classroom if more money were available.

reduce the size of classes in their school. In contrast, over half the American teachers would use such funds to reduce class size. What did the teachers consider the ideal class size? The average number of children suggested by the American teachers was 20; both Chinese and Japanese teachers on the average proposed 29 as the ideal number.

Teachers were also asked to make recommendations for spending extra funds if the money were given for use in the teacher's own classroom. Their recommendations differed from those made when the focus was the school (see the bottom panel of Fig. 14). Dominating all other recommendations was the purchase of new academic equipment, such as books and classroom materials. Minneapolis teachers no longer were as interested in reducing the size of their classes, and Taipei and Sendai teachers were less willing to use the funds to initiate new nonacademic activities. Teachers' priorities were to improve the equipment available to them for teaching and to provide children with more opportunities at school for interesting and beneficial activities that were outside traditional academic subjects. Few teachers would use extra funds for personal advantage. In fact, only six of the 120 teachers suggested that they would use additional funds for improving teachers' salaries.

CONCLUDING COMMENTS

The interviews did not produce a picture of mothers troubled about their child's education. Those in Minneapolis and Sendai tended to believe that more emphasis on academic subjects, particularly reading, would be appropriate, whereas Chinese mothers were more likely to suggest increased emphasis on nonacademic subjects. A majority of the mothers did not believe that their child had encountered problems in learning to read or do mathematics. When problems did arise, mothers in all three cities believed that these should be handled within the home rather than at school.

In assisting children and coping with school problems, Minneapolis mothers tended to stress emotional and motivational solutions, such as becoming more involved, supportive, or enthusiastic and creating a stable and nurturant relationship with the child. We believe that this approach may have a crucial defect: despite making children feel better, such solutions fail to provide the knowledge and skills that are instrumental in improving performance.

The data clarify the implications of the term *kyoiku mama*, which is often applied to Japanese mothers. The "education mom" is the person who assumes responsibility for supervising and directing the child's learning, not for being an out-of-school teacher. Japanese mothers mentioned efforts to help their child, but they did this no more frequently than the Chinese and American mothers. However, much more often than the Chinese and American mothers, Japanese mothers tended to organize the child's environment so that it was comfortable and equipped with the resources necessary for effective learning. American mothers suggested that they would help their child, but they were more likely to emphasize the importance of offering more encouragement to their child and becoming more involved with their child. Chinese mothers also relied heavily on encouragement as a means of fostering high levels of academic achievement.

When parental help was given to Minneapolis and Sendai children, it tended to be ameliorative in that more time was given to low achievers. In Taipei, there was no relation between the time spent in helping the child and the child's level of achievement, and the majority of the children were helped with schoolwork by the whole family. Minneapolis mothers believed that they play a more important role in their child's education than did Taipei or Sendai mothers, who gave a greater importance to teachers.

Teachers in all three locations assigned similar rankings to various factors that might contribute to children's performance in school and disagreed primarily about the importance of strict discipline, study groups, recitation, teacher availability after class, and homework. More Minneapolis and Sendai teachers than Taipei teachers described problems in teaching.

XII. DISCUSSION

The superiority in mathematics and science of Japanese and Chinese junior high school and high school students was established in several earlier studies. Our research has revealed that the relative disadvantage of American children in mathematics and reading is evident as early as the first grade. When differences in performance appear as early as the child's first grade of school, factors at home as well as at school must be responsible. It is hard to tell whether similar results would have been obtained in a comparable cross-cultural study 50 years ago. Whether the lower scores of the American children relative to the Chinese and Japanese children signify a worsening of the status of American students or simply more rapid progress in other societies is impossible to determine. Whatever the interpretation, the fact remains that there is a need to understand the bases of these differences and to make efforts to reduce them.

METHODOLOGY

We have been asked about the degree to which each city is representative of its culture. Minneapolis's economic prosperity, emphasis on education, ethnic homogeneity, and high status as a cultural center preclude its being considered as a truly representative American city. We can assume only that the selection of another city would have resulted in even more extreme sets of differences from Taipei and Sendai than those we obtained. Indeed, we and our colleagues have found this to be the case in our current research, in which we are comparing the performance of children in Chicago with that of children in Taipei, Sendai, and Beijing (Stevenson et al., in press; Stigler et al., in press). Moreover, we are finding that differences among white, black, and Hispanic children are less than the differences in performance between any one of these groups and the performance of Chinese and Japanese children.

Taipei and Sendai are probably more representative of other large cities in Taiwan and Japan than is Minneapolis of the United States. There is likely to be greater similarity in educational practices among cities when a central government prescribes such things as the school curricula and when a population consists of a single ethnic group than when decisions are decentralized and the population is diverse, as is the case in the United States.

We encountered no serious obstacles in obtaining representative samples of children in each city. Parents were very cooperative in allowing their children to be tested and interviewed and in agreeing to be interviewed themselves. We believe our sampling procedures resulted in representative samples of the populations of children residing in these three cities.

Materials were developed especially for the study by persons familiar with the cultures in which they would be used. We believe that we minimized the problems inherent in cross-cultural studies. We constructed test items and interview questions that would be as comparable as possible in the three languages. Because all the materials for the study were prepared by native speakers of each language, we avoided the problem of working in only one language and then attempting to find the closest approximations in the other two languages. If the content of an item was not satisfactory to other professionals in the three cultures, it was not included.

We had been warned that it would be difficult to obtain reliable information from interviews with mothers who were not experienced in using rating scales or in answering open-ended questions. This proved not to be the case, even though this was typically the first time that the mothers had been interviewed. The relevance of the questions for their daily experiences and the fact that the interviews were conducted by residents of the cities in which the mothers themselves resided enabled us to avoid this methodological pitfall.

READING AND MATHEMATICS

The Minneapolis children did not fare as badly in reading as they did in mathematics. Literacy is a goal of educational systems in all societies, but it seems to be the paramount goal of American elementary school education. Why this should be the case and why so much time is spent on reading is not clear. Perhaps in a society of immigrants such as has existed in the United States, major importance is placed on being able to speak and read the language of the new country. Moreover, American parents may not acknowledge the role of mathematics in their child's later education and work, and American teachers may not like to teach mathematics. At any rate, reading was greatly emphasized and was the subject above all others that the Minneapolis mothers believed should receive even more emphasis.

Some of the American children did well in reading, but there was a disproportionately large number of poor readers—children who would be classified not as reading disabled but simply as slow in learning to read. The greater tendency of the American than of the Chinese and Japanese children to be overrepresented among both the poorest and the best readers appears to be attributable in part to the use of an alphabetic writing system. An alphabet, in contrast to a logographic system that uses symbols such as Chinese characters, makes it possible for children to sound out words that they have not been taught to read. The alphabet has this advantage, but it also has disadvantages, such as the imperfect relation between symbol and sound. Some children learn the rules for sounding out words early and are able to read new words; others are slow in learning these rules and soon fall below their grade level in reading skill.

The American children's weakness in mathematics is not surprising when so little emphasis is placed on mathematics by both teachers and parents. Minneapolis mothers thought mathematics was not especially difficult, they believed that their children did not experience problems in learning mathematics, and they seldom recommended placing greater emphasis on instruction in mathematics. Their children agreed that mathematics was not difficult. Indeed, the mathematics taught in American elementary schools is easy. Analyses of the mathematics textbooks used by the children supported this conclusion (Stigler et al., 1982). Although the curricula in the three cities contained approximately equal numbers of mathematical concepts and skills, similar concepts were introduced earlier in the Japanese than in the American curriculum. The Chinese curriculum was not more advanced than the American curriculum, but over three times as many hours were spent in Taipei each week than in Minneapolis in mastering its content.

Achievement in reading and mathematics had a different meaning in the three cultures. The Chinese and Japanese children were more likely to consider themselves bright if they were good in mathematics than if they were good in reading. The American children believed that brightness was more highly related to their reading ability. Similarly, success in school was more strongly defined by the Chinese and Japanese children in terms of their performance in mathematics but by the American children in terms of both reading and mathematics.

TIME ON TASK

Schools appeared to be more efficiently managed and organized according to the developmental needs of children in Taipei and Sendai than was the case in Minneapolis. This may seem paradoxical to those who have read about high-pressured Asian schools, but educational authorities in Taiwan and Japan arrange the academic programs so that they are in accord with the needs of children at different developmental levels. First graders spend less time in school than fifth graders. Frequent recesses meet the need for relaxation after attending to schoolwork. Efforts are made to make school an interesting place by providing many after-school activities.

Although the amount of time allocated each day to core academic subjects does not greatly exceed that of schools in the United States, we found in our extensive observational study that time was used more efficiently in Chinese and Japanese schools. Teachers were vigorous and innovative, lessons were well organized and captured the children's attention, and homework assignments were thoughtfully planned. Chinese and Japanese children benefit from the greater amounts of time spent on academic activities, not because they have more chances for drill and repetition, but because the time is spent in interesting and productive ways. This was reflected in children's attitudes; Taipei and Sendai children were less likely than Minneapolis children to want to stay home from school.

In discussions of educational reform, it has been suggested that higher levels of achievement would be obtained if the school day and the school year were extended in the United States and the amount of homework were increased. The risk exists that increasing the amount of time spent in academic activities without modifying the content of the curriculum and the manner of instruction might further depress American children's interest in school and increase their dislike of homework. Greater time on task is not the primary basis for the high achievement of Chinese and Japanese children. The answer lies instead in the high quality of the experiences that fill this time. Nor is the success of Asian elementary school children due to attendance at after-school classes in core subjects. Attendance at after-school classes in academic subjects such as reading and mathematics was infrequent in all three cities.

INTEREST IN ACADEMIC ACHIEVEMENT

It is common knowledge that education is highly prized in Chinese and Japanese cultures. Americans are also interested in education, but they seem to have different goals from those found in Asia. Our results reveal some of the ways in which these interests and goals are transformed into concrete forms of behavior. The American mothers did not require their child to demonstrate high levels of academic achievement for them to be satisfied. Nor were they dissatisfied unless the child's performance was notably below average. Our impression is that the Minneapolis mothers wanted schools to provide experiences that led to more general cognitive development defined by improved learning and problem-solving ability rather than to mastery of the curriculum. From the perspective of these American mothers, it is better for children to be bright than to be good students. The situation is very different in Taiwan and Japan. Going to school and doing well academically are the children's two main responsibilities.

Chinese and Japanese families dedicate themselves to their child's schoolwork. This was evidenced by the space, funds, and time allocated to the child. The child was relieved of obligations to assist the family through chores and was given greater freedom once the day's homework was completed. As long as a child is successful in school, few demands are made in other domains. The American families did not show the same commitment to academic achievement. The American mothers did not mention academic activity often as something their child was involved in after school, and they did not spend large amounts of time helping their child, especially if he or she was doing well.

The meaning of "doing well" differed in the eyes of the Chinese and Japanese mothers. Academic performance dominated the attention of Chinese mothers. Their primary criterion for success in elementary school was the child's grades. They expected grades to show continuous improvement, in relation both to those obtained by other children and to the child's own past performance. The greatest concern of Japanese parents is that their child learn what is necessary for passing entrance examinations. Japanese mothers know that grades have little relevance for gaining admission to prestigious schools and that all decisions about admission are based on the scores on entrance examinations.

INVOLVEMENT OF THE FAMILY

Chinese.—Americans have been greatly interested in Japan's accomplishments in education, and discussions of educational reforms often center on the Japanese situation. Data from this study suggest that the accomplishments of Chinese children are even more remarkable, especially in view of the conditions under which they occur. Schools and classrooms in Taipei are crowded, teachers generally have no more than the equivalent of a junior college education, and parents, especially mothers, are not highly educated. Kindergarten education is not universal, and Chinese children enter the first grade with fewer academic skills than do American and Japanese children. In spite of these obstacles, the Chinese children made spectacular gains in achievement during elementary school.

The socialization of Chinese children resulted in close concordance between the beliefs of the mother, the teacher, and the child. Children accept the philosophy that the major path to success is through effort, and they incorporate their parents' beliefs about the importance of academic achievement. They enter school with a clear purpose and a willingness to work hard. Because they have internalized the value of learning, their motivation remains high throughout the elementary school years. In contrast to American and Japanese families, where mothers assume primary responsibility for assisting children with their schoolwork, the whole Chinese family participates in this effort. Parents play an important role in supervising their children's schoolwork, and even mothers with little education perform this task effectively. Between parents, older siblings, and other relatives, there is usually someone available in Chinese families to assist children when they encounter problems in schoolwork. The task for all Chinese children, even those who are not doing well in school, is clear: they must achieve at least the minimal level of performance set for children in their grade level.

Japanese.—The data from this study dispel the Western image of the Japanese mother as a pushy, demanding, home-bound tutor. It appears more appropriate to describe her as one who attempts to provide a nurturant and protected atmosphere for learning. She is ready to assist her child in doing homework if she can, but her major goals are to promote the child's interest and involvement in school and to make sure that the child has a comfortable environment at home. Our data depict a mother making realistic, sensitive evaluations of her child's strengths and weaknesses and striving to lead her child to independent pursuit of knowledge. She minimizes her contribution to the child's education and, even more than her Chinese counterpart, stresses the utility of hard work. Neither the Japanese nor the Chinese mother denies the potential contribution of innate differences in abilities; they stress, instead, the impossibility of the child's realizing his or her full potential without strong and sustained effort.

Japanese mothers are unrelenting in their self-sacrifice and dedication to their children. They are not critical or harsh, but they do maintain very high standards. It is not direct demands from the mother but the anticipation of later entrance examinations that leads Japanese children to feel pressure about their schoolwork. By the fifth grade, Japanese children begin to indicate some dislike for school, a lack of confidence about their future, and a rather pessimistic view of themselves.

American.—In contrast to an educational philosophy that places strong emphasis on promoting the development of internal sources of motivation about schoolwork, our data indicate that the American children depended on external sources of motivation. They completed their assignments because they were told to do so in order to meet parental wishes. They believed that they were living up to the expectations of their teachers and parents. Mothers were satisfied with their child's current level of performance, even though they believed that their child potentially could do better. Mothers saw their role as providing emotional support to their child and believed that they made an important contribution to their child's education. When their child had difficulties, they said that they should be encouraging and involved, in an attempt to increase their child's interest in schoolwork. Social interaction between parents and children appeared to be greater among the American families than among those in Taiwan and Japan, but the interaction was likely to be about topics other than school.

The value that Minneapolis mothers placed on cognitive development was manifested in many ways, including reading to their child, taking their child on excursions, and attempting to provide other experiences at home that could stimulate cognitive growth. Their optimistic and positive views of their children did not closely match what we learned from the results of our tests. Despite their highly favorable evaluations of their child's general cognitive abilities, we found no overall differences by the fifth grade in the cognitive abilities of American, Chinese, and Japanese children, and, despite the mothers' belief that their child was progressing well in school, we found low achievement relative to the other cultures.

The data lead to the impression that American mothers may be dedicated to the child's development during his or her preschool years but that they abdicate some of these responsibilities to the teacher once the child enters school. This trend is opposite from that which occurs in Chinese and Japanese families, where the preschool years are a time of freedom and indulgence and there is no great concern about the child's learning academic skills. From the time that the child enters school, life for the Chinese and Japanese child becomes purposeful; the child, the parents, and the teachers begin the serious task of education. The more years the children are in school, the stronger the emphasis on academic activities becomes. For American children, the transition to elementary school is a less notable event. From the time they enter school, their lives are not encumbered by strong demands for academic excellence or homework, and there is little increase in demands during the 6 years of elementary school. The American parents found it acceptable for elementary school children to play, watch television, and do little academic work outside school. The time spent by American children in recreational activities after school may be a consequence of their more limited opportunities for social interaction and play at school, restrictions that result from infrequent recesses and the lack of opportunities for after-school activities at school.

STANDARDS AND EVALUATIONS

Two factors that work strongly against high achievement by American children are the low academic standards held by parents and the overestimations that parents make of their children's abilities. If a parent believes that a child is doing well and conveys this impression to the child, the child may see no purpose in studying harder. American children gave themselves the highest ratings on their ability in reading and mathematics, brightness, and scholastic performance, and Japanese children gave themselves the lowest ratings. This may indicate excessive confidence on the part of the American children. However, ratings by the mothers followed the same pattern. In the eyes of mothers in all three cities, the average child was above average. But the degree of bias was much greater among the American mothers than among the Japanese. These biases extended to their evaluations of their own abilities; the most positive self-evaluations were made by the American mothers.

The Taipei and Sendai mothers expected more of their children and raised their standards as their children progressed through elementary school. In contrast, Minneapolis mothers demanded less and less from their children. It is not clear why the American mothers overestimated their children's abilities and accomplishments and held such low standards for satisfaction about academic achievement. One possible reason is that they were more worried than the Chinese and Japanese mothers that increased demands for academic achievement would be psychologically unhealthy for their child. One of the most commonly voiced criticisms by Americans about Chinese and Japanese students is that they must experience great stress from studying so hard and that they lack vigor, creativity, and joy in learning. We found no grounds for these fears in the many visits we have made to elementary school classrooms in Taiwan and Japan. Although our observational methods did not include ratings of such activities, it is our impression that Chinese and Japanese elementary school classrooms, contrary to common stereotypes, are characterized by frequent interchange between teacher and students, enthusiastic participation by the students, and the frequent use of problems that require novel and innovative solutions.

In fact, pressures felt by American children may actually be higher than those experienced by Chinese and Japanese children, but the origins for such pressures may be unrelated to school. The American teachers suggested that children in their classrooms had a great many personal problems. One teacher stated it this way: "Sometimes I feel that trying to help some of the kids is almost hopeless. Their lives at home are such a mess that they can't function well at school. I try so hard, but. . . ." There may be some basis, therefore, for the concern of American parents about the possible negative effects if the pressure on academic achievement were increased.

INNATE ABILITIES

The relative lack of interest of the American mothers in academic activities may stem partly from the degree to which they emphasize innate abilities as a determinant of performance. Would Chinese and Japanese parents and teachers be willing to devote so much time and energy to the education of their children if they did not believe that the effort expended by themselves and by their children would not yield important results for their children? Would Chinese and Japanese children demonstrate such intense dedication to their schoolwork if they did not believe that hard work was highly valued in their society and constituted the major route to academic achievement?

An extreme interpretation of a nativist philosophy leads to two conclusions: first, that children of high ability need not work hard to achieve and, second, that children of low ability will not achieve regardless of how hard they work. The remarkable success of Japanese and Chinese students appears to be due in part to renunciation of these views.

Tracking does not exist within Chinese and Japanese schools. There is no grouping within classes according to level of ability, and there are no special education teachers or special classes for slow learners. At the elementary school level, teachers hold the sincere belief that all children are capable of mastering the curriculum and that academic success is within the grasp of all children if they apply themselves wholeheartedly to their schoolwork. Children are believed to differ not so much in their potential level of attainment as in the rate at which they approach this level. Slow learners are expected to benefit from the good models provided by rapid learners, and rapid learners are expected to solidify their understanding through the added practice and experience given to the class for the benefit of children who learn more slowly. It should be pointed out that these procedures carry with them the possibility of problems. Highly able students are not allowed to progress to the levels of which they are capable, and, in order to accommodate slower learners, there may have to be more repetition and drill than most children need. The large size of the classes increases the difficulty of ascertaining how well individual children are comprehending the lessons, and the lack of specialists such as special education teachers and school psychologists sometimes makes it difficult for teachers to meet the needs of students needing special help.

American teachers worry about meeting the needs of each individual child. This, together with the emphasis on the importance of individual differences in innate abilities, justifies the separation of children into subgroups and special classes. Arguments may be made for tracking, such as that it provides more time for slow learners and more challenges for fast learners, but it deprives children of different levels of ability from learning from each other and stigmatizes children in the lower tracks. Tracking may in some cases yield a false security to those in the higher tracks that is not conducive to maximum effort. A second important consequence of the emphasis on meeting the needs of individual children is that children in American classrooms receive less instruction than do Chinese and Japanese children. The time spent by the teacher working with one child or one ability group deprives the rest of the students of time with the teacher. If guidance and instruction by the teacher are considered more important for academic achievement than seat work done by children without supervision, it would be readily predicted that American children's achievement would be below that of children in classrooms with procedures similar to those used in Taiwan and Japan.

CONCLUSIONS

The poor performance of the American children in this study was due to numerous factors, many of which are neither elusive nor subtle. Some of the most salient reasons for poor performance appear to be the following: insufficient time and emphasis were devoted to academic activities; children's academic achievement was not a widely shared goal; children and their parents overestimated the children's accomplishments; parental standards for achievement were low; there was little direct involvement of parents in children's schoolwork; and an emphasis on nativism may have undermined the belief that all but seriously disabled children should be able to master the content of the elementary school curriculum.

REFERENCES

Azuma, H., Kashiwagi, K., & Hess, R. D. (1981). *Hahaoya no taido koudo to kodomo no chiteki hattatsu* (The effect of mother's attitude and behavior on the cognitive development of the child: A U.S.-Japanese comparison). Tokyo: University of Tokyo Press.
Bond, M. H. (1986). *The psychology of the Chinese people.* Hong Kong: Oxford University Press.
Christopher, R. C. (1983). *The Japanese mind: The Goliath explained.* New York: Linden.
Coleman, J. S., Campbell, E. Q., Hobson, C. J., McPartland, J., Mood, A. M., Weinfeld, F. D., & York, R. L. (1966). *Equality of educational opportunity.* Washington, DC: U.S. Government Printing Office.
Comber, L. C., & Keeves, J. (1973). *Science achievement in nineteen countries.* New York: Wiley.
Cummings, W. K. (1980). *Education and equality in Japan.* Princeton, NJ: Princeton University Press.
DeVos, G. (1973). *Socialization for achievement.* Berkeley: University of California Press.
Duke, B. (1986). *The Japanese school: Lessons for industrial America.* New York: Praeger.
Entwisle, D. R., & Hayduk, L. A. (1978). *Too great expectations: The academic outlook of young children.* Baltimore: Johns Hopkins University Press.
Garden, R. A. (1987). The second IEA mathematics study. *Comparative Education Review,* **31,** 47–68.
Goodlad, J. I. (1984). *A place called school: Prospects for the future.* New York: McGraw-Hill.
Hess, R. D., Holloway, S. D., Dickson, P. W., & Price, G. G. (1984). Maternal variables as predictors of children's school readiness and later achievement in vocabulary and mathematics in sixth grade. *Child Development,* **55,** 1902–1912.
Kessen, W. (Ed.). (1975). *Childhood in China.* New Haven, CT: Yale University Press.
Lebra, T. S., & Lebra, W. J. (Eds.). (1974). *Japanese culture and behavior.* Honolulu: University of Hawaii Press.
Lee, S. Y., Ichikawa, V., & Stevenson, H. W. (1987). Beliefs and achievement in mathematics and reading: A cross-national study of Chinese, Japanese and American children and their mothers. In D. Kleiber & M. Maehr (Eds.), *Advances in achievement and motivation: Enhancing motivation* (pp. 149–179). Greenwich, CT: JAI.
Lewis, C. (1984). Cooperation and control in Japanese nursery schools. *Comparative Education Review,* **28,** 69–84.
Lynn, R. (1982). IQ in Japan and the United States shows a growing disparity. *Nature,* **297,** 222–223.
Lynn, R. (1988). *Educational achievement in Japan: Lessons for the West.* Armonk, NY: Sharpe.
Lynn, R., & Hampson, S. (1986). Intellectual abilities of Japanese children: An assessment

of 2½–8½-year-olds derived from the McCarthy Scales of Children's Abilities. *Intelligence, 10,* 41–58.

McKnight, C. C., Crosswhite, F. J., Dossey, J. A., Kifer, E., Swafford, J. O., Travers, K. J., & Cooney, T. J. (1987). *The underachieving curriculum: Assessing U.S. school mathematics from an international perspective.* Champaign, IL: Stipes.

Miller, S. (1988). Parents' beliefs about children's cognitive development. *Child Development, 59,* 259–285.

Ministry of Education. (1988). *Educational statistics in the Republic of China.* Taipei: Ministry of Education.

Ministry of Education, Science, and Culture. (1978). *Education in Japan: A graphic presentation.* Tokyo: Gyosei.

Miura, I. T., Kim, C. C., Chang, C. M., & Okamoto, Y. (1988). Effects of language characteristics on children's cognitive representation of number: Cross-national comparisons. *Child Development, 59,* 1445–1450.

Munro, D. J. (1977). *The concept of man in contemporary China.* Ann Arbor: University of Michigan Press.

Paris, S. G., Olson, G. M., & Stevenson, H. W. (1983). *Learning and motivation in the classroom.* Hillsdale, NJ: Erlbaum.

Rohlen, T. P. (1983). *Japan's high schools.* Berkeley: University of California Press.

Stanovich, K. (1987). Introduction. *Merrill-Palmer Quarterly,* **33.**

Stevenson, H. W., & Azuma, H. (1983). IQ in Japan and the United States: Methodological problems in Lynn's analysis. *Nature,* **306,** 291–292.

Stevenson, H. W., Azuma, H., & Hakuta, K. (1986). *Child development and education in Japan.* New York: Freeman.

Stevenson, H. W., & Bartsch, K. (in press). An analysis of Japanese and American textbooks in mathematics. In R. Leestma & H. Walberg (Eds.), *Japanese education.* Washington, DC: U.S. Government Printing Office.

Stevenson, H. W., Lee, S. Y., Chen, C., Lummis, J., Stigler, J., Fan, L., & Ge, F. (in press). Mathematics achievement of children in China and the United States. *Child Development.*

Stevenson, H. W., Stigler, J. W., Lee, S., Lucker, W., Kitamura, S., & Hsu, C. (1985). Cognitive performance and academic achievement of Japanese, Chinese, and American children. *Child Development,* **56,** 718–734.

Stevenson, H. W., Stigler, J. W., Lucker, G. W., Lee, S., Hsu, C., & Kitamura, S. (1982). Reading disabilities: The case of Chinese, Japanese and English. *Child Development,* **53,** 1164–1181.

Stevenson, H. W., Stigler, J. W., Lucker, G. W., Lee, S., Hsu, C. C., & Kitamura, S. (1987). Classroom behavior and achievement of Japanese, Chinese, and American children. In R. Glaser (Ed.), *Advances in instructional psychology* (Vol. **3,** pp. 153–204). Hillsdale, NJ: Erlbaum.

Stigler, J. W., Lee, S., Lucker, G. W., & Stevenson, H. W. (1982). Curriculum and achievement in mathematics: A study of elementary school children in Japan, Taiwan, and the United States. *Journal of Educational Psychology,* **74,** 315–322.

Stigler, J. W., Lee, S. Y., & Stevenson, H. W. (1987). Mathematics classrooms in Japan, Taiwan, and the United States. *Child Development,* **58,** 1272–1285.

Stigler, J. W., Lee, S. Y., & Stevenson, H. W. (in press). Mathematics knowledge of Japanese, Chinese, and American elementary school children. *National Council of Teachers of Mathematics Monographs.*

U.S. Department of Education. (1988). *Youth indicators: Trends in the well-being of American youth.* Washington, DC: U.S. Government Printing Office.

MONOGRAPHS

Vogel, E. F. (1979). *Japan as no. 1: Lessons for America.* Cambridge, MA: Harvard University Press.
Watson, B. (1967). *Basic writings of Mo Tzu, Hsun Tzu, and Han Fei Tzu.* New York: Columbia University Press.
White, M. (1987). *The Japanese challenge: A commitment to children.* New York: Free Press.
Wilson, R. W. (1979). *Learning to be Chinese: The political socialization of children in Taiwan.* Cambridge, MA: MIT Press.

ACKNOWLEDGMENTS

The conduct of this study was supported by National Institute of Mental Health grant MH 33529. The writing of this report was supported by a grant from the National Science Foundation (MDR 8751390). We are deeply grateful to the children, teachers, parents, and school officials who made it possible for us to conduct this study, to the interviewers and examiners who worked so diligently, and to Ai-lan Tsao, our coordinator in Taipei; Ada Hegion, Elizabeth Clarke, and Darlene Stealey, our coordinators in Minneapolis; and Susumu Kimura and the late Tadahisa Kato, our project coordinators in Sendai. Many others were involved in this research. We especially want to thank David Crandall, Veronica Ichikawa, Richard Goldberg, Mayumi Homma, G. William Lucker, Kuniaki Nagai, Kyung-sun Lim, Max Lummis, Akemi Shishido, Shu-jen Su, and David Uttal, who were extremely helpful. Catherine Arnott has offered suggestions for clarifying the writing and helped us prepare the manuscript for publication.

COMMENTARY

TOWARD THE CULTURAL PSYCHOLOGY OF MATHEMATICAL COGNITION

GIYOO HATANO

This *Monograph* reports on the third step of the first study conducted by Harold Stevenson and his associates in their long-range and ambitious research program. In the first step, these investigators demonstrated that large differences in mathematics achievement existed between the United States and two Asian countries, China-Taiwan and Japan, even at the elementary school level. Because of their careful methodology as well as skillful data presentation, these findings have become widely known not only among scholars but also among lay people concerned with education. In the second step, they observed students and teachers from the three cultures in their classrooms in order to establish what cross-cultural differences in the students' school experience might explain some of the observed differences in achievement.

Although Stevenson et al. state a relatively modest goal for the third step, namely, "to describe the contexts in which different levels of achievement occur" (p. 1), it was certainly an attempt to identify out-of-school causal factors for the impressive cross-national differences in mathematics achievement that they had reported earlier. Through interviews with children and their mothers, the authors examined five clusters of variables as candidates for sociocultural conditions facilitating achievement: emphasis on academic achievement, involvement of parents and other members of the society, realism in evaluation, moderately high standards of performance, and emphasis on effort. Implicitly, the central question addressed in the *Monograph* is how the differences in mathematics achievement are socioculturally produced. In fact, on the last page the authors write, "The poor performance of the American children in this study *was due* to numerous factors. . . . Some of the most salient *reasons* for poor performance appear to be ..." (p. 103; italics added). In other words, the authors believe that they are offering some causal factors for the differences.

In this Commentary, I will assess the contribution of Stevenson et al.'s research program to theories of mathematical development, focusing on material presented in this *Monograph*. I will also try to suggest promising future directions for their program.

Specifying the Nature of Mathematics Achievement

Although it documented dramatic cross-national differences in mathematics achievement, the first step of Stevenson et al.'s first study did not greatly advance our understanding of the development of mathematical cognition. Most researchers in the field of mathematical cognition and/or instruction are aware of its findings but take them as mostly irrelevant to their activities.

This indifference arises from the fact that the subjects' mathematical knowledge has not been analyzed in detail by Stevenson and his associates. Their cross-national comparison of the distributions of the average scores of classrooms makes the differences in achievement eye catching, but it does not illuminate how children differed in the three cultures in terms of possession and use of knowledge.

Since their first study generated so much data, it is easily understandable that those data require a long time to be fully analyzed. So far, only total scores pertaining to "calculation" and to "problem solving" have been published. More informative data based on error analyses across cultures, characterizations of items that show large versus negligible cultural differences, and so on have as yet to be reported.

A more serious limitation lies in the nature of the test that was used. It was designed to be a tool for "fair" overall comparison, and, for this purpose, it was constructed with the greatest care. Almost all test items were based on content common to the curricula of all three countries, and the test contained a representative sampling of important topics. However, it was not designed to determine what knowledge students actually had, what of it they could use promptly, and so on. It contained almost no items "novel" for the subjects, that is, dealing with concepts that had not been taught. This made it impossible to assess and compare how much students in each culture could transfer their knowledge with either no or minimal instruction. These pieces of missing information might be supplied by a series of (smaller-scale) assessments and interviews, and apparently some have already been collected in the course of the second study (see Stigler & Perry, 1988). Reanalyses of the test performance data using only preselected relevant items may also be informative.

At a minimum, to make the investigation of causal factors systematic, generalizable, and interesting, some conceptual characterization of the differences in achievement is needed. Without it, there is no theoretical basis for choosing among candidate factors. Since effective conditions for acquisition may vary according to what is to be acquired, even empirical generalizations will be impossible unless the nature of the differences is clarified. If not informed by analysis of the cognitive outcome, no more than some crude version of reinforcement theory—such as, "The competence is acquired because it is expected and rewarded"—can be offered as a basis for explaining the observed differences in achievement.

Let me rely on Resnick (1989) to derive a framework for such a characterization. According to this author, whereas the acquisition of "certain fundamental mathematical ideas" occurs early and is perhaps "universal," many children have great difficulty in learning school mathematics, probably because of its formal, symbol-manipulating nature. If so, then we can offer two competing interpretations of the cross-national differences in mathematics achievement observed by Stevenson et al.: either many more Asian students can apply their intuition to school mathematics, or, though unable to apply intuition (and thus unable to achieve conceptual understanding), they are much better at symbol manipulation.

Which interpretation is correct, or, if both are correct to some extent, which is the more accurate understanding? This question serves to guide the discussion that follows in this Commentary; so far, Stevenson et al.'s research program has not provided conclusive evidence needed for an answer.

Cultural Imposition of Selected Values

At this stage of research on learning, it is possible and even necessary to attempt to identify the effective conditions for learning and instruction of such types of cognitive outcomes as efficiency in the execution of a fixed set of skills, the conceptual knowledge needed for solving novel problems, and so on—in other words, to construct a sociocultural version of "the conditions of learning" (Gagné, 1965). Understanding the "effective conditions" not only has practical value but also illuminates the process by which the outcome is achieved (Price & Hatano, in press). The third step of Stevenson et al.'s research program provides a substantial contribution to such an enterprise. If future analyses show that Asian students are primarily better at mathematics qua symbol manipulations, then it is intriguing as a study of how culture enforces acquisition of the competence that it values but that has no intrinsic significance for its members.

Stevenson et al.'s conclusions provide a simple, convincing story explaining why the Asian countries produce high mathematics achievement in their children. Asian culture emphasizes and gives priority to mathematical learning; high achievement in mathematics is taken by mature members of the culture to be an important goal for its less mature members. The former assess the latter's accomplishments carefully and, whenever help is needed, are willing to give it so that they will accomplish more; it is assumed by all that effort makes a difference in the level of one's accomplishments.

These conclusions suggest two important generalizations. First, as has been aptly pointed out by Goodnow (in press), a culture is not necessarily benign or benevolent—it may impose selected values on its members, especially its less mature members. Second, this process of imposition need not, however, take a dictatorial form. As noted by Stevenson et al., Japanese mothers, known as *kyoiku mama,* attempt "to provide a nurturant and protected atmosphere for learning" (p. 99). Mediating individuals and groups appear warm, kind, and respectful of individual will. They socialize less mature members in a subtle way—making best use of their closeness, they lead them to internalize the cultural values. Once these values are internalized, the motivation to pursue them comes from within the individual.

Let me cite two more examples of this type of cultural imposition so as to show the generality of the sociocultural conditions that were observed by Stevenson et al. The first is the acquisition of the standard orthography by Japanese children. As noted in this *Monograph,* Japanese children have to learn more than 2,000 *kanji* (Chinese characters) and their complicated uses in order to read and write in a mature fashion. This takes many years, whereas the acquisition of *kana* syllabaries, by which any Japanese word can be expressed, is very easy. Why, then, do the children acquire that many *kanji?* It is because the Japanese culture values their use. More specifically, being able to read and write many words in *kanji* is regarded as a sign of intellectual maturity (Hatano, 1986), and parents, as mature members of the culture, pay close attention to their children's mastery of *kanji* and are willing to help them as needed.

National sports provide another example. When a country has a national sport as part of its culture—that is, contests that almost all members find interesting to participate in or watch—the team representing that country tends to be strong, even if its population is small. Soccer in Paraguay or rugby in Fiji are such instances. This means that, if we were somehow to measure that country's children's skill for playing the given sport, their scores would be very high; since the culture values being good at it, considerable time is allocated to practicing the sport, and peers, if not parents, pay close attention to less mature members' mastery, are willing to help, and so on.

What is common to the three examples that I have just described is that children have almost no other choice than to seek mastery of such culturally prescribed skills. In contrast, there are also many skills that are viewed as culturally provided alternatives and for which freedom of choice is allowed. I think that school mathematics is a national (in the sense used above) intellectual pursuit in Asian countries, but not in the United States. Whereas students cannot escape from it in the former, in the latter they are told (at least implicitly) that, if they are poor at or dislike mathematics, they are free to seek achievement in some other area.

This difference in whether the acquisition of skill in school mathematics is compulsory or optional seems related to the emphasis placed on effort. Ten years ago, I claimed that the Japanese might be characterized by their belief in effort: "While Japanese people think that effort makes a difference everywhere (i.e., even when one lacks ability), Americans tend to regard effort meaningful only insofar as one is smart (bright) or talented enough in the field" (Hatano, 1982b, p. 58). I even claimed that this belief in effort facilitated students' ability for calculation (Hatano, 1982a). Now I would like to propose a more "domain-specific" assumption, namely, that, whereas people generally tend to assign much more importance to effort in regard to skills that every member of the society is expected to acquire, ability may be considered more important in the case of optional skills. It is likely that the American culture allows its members to decline gaining competence in more domains than its Japanese or other Asian counterparts, permitting Americans to preserve their belief in ability without being fatalists.

A limitation of the conclusions suggested here by Stevenson et al. is that the view of the cultural influences on children's competence is one sided. I believe that culture not only imposes its values but also realizes the potential of its members by encouraging exploration, exchange of ideas, participation in the community of mature members, and so on. This second aspect of culture also seems relevant to the development of mathematical comprehension; for instance, parents' encouragement and responsiveness to the numerical and quantitative reasoning of their children may enhance the latter's construction of mathematical knowledge. Thus, the limitation imposed by not considering the benign or "supportive" aspects of the culture would be serious insofar as the cross-national differences in mathematics achievement reflect differences in mathematical understanding because the development of such understanding is advanced more by encouraging learners to reason than by pressing them to perfect their problem-solving skills.

An ideal design for a future study is to assess children' skills at manipulation of symbols and the extent of their mathematical understanding separately and to correlate these measures with variables representing supportive as well as "imposing" aspects of the culture. This would reveal the extent to which effective conditions vary according to the nature of the cognitive outcomes that underlie high achievement in mathematics.

It should be noted that questions concerning the supportive aspects of the culture were not included in the interviews, even though Stevenson et al. did not commit themselves expressly to any theory in seeking out all variables that might influence mathematics achievement. Despite their attempt at objectivity and comprehensiveness, either consciously or unconsciously they in fact adopted a version of reinforcement theory, probably because detailed analyses of high mathematics achievement were not available to provide them with other cues in considering the processes of acquisition.

Can Asian Countries Be Taken as a Model?

Stevenson has long been interested in seeing developmental research make a contribution in setting social policy. Accordingly, this third step of Stevenson et al.'s research program aims not only at understanding the causes of cross-national differences in mathematics achievement but also at reducing them; more specifically, in assisting the United States to catch up with the Asian countries.

High incidence of low achievement in mathematics can be likened to a high incidence of some disease. If so, is it a disease of deficiency, like beriberi? In other words, is its cause singular, and is it prevented or cured by a specific procedure? In the same way as beriberi is caused by the lack of vitamin B1 and, without knowing precisely how or why, is prevented by eating rice boiled with barley, is low mathematics achievement caused by one sociocultural factor, and can it be greatly reduced by manipulating that factor?

Alternatively, is this "disease" more like stomach cancer, with many causes and mediating variables? Although epidemiology has suggested a number of foods as candidates for its "major causes," the removal of any single food cannot have a dramatic effect. We Japanese used to be urged to eat more Western food because the incidence of stomach cancer is much lower in Europe and the United States. The recommended change did take place—not because of the recommendation itself but because of a general Westernization of society—and it has proved to some extent effective in reducing the incidence of such cancer. However, reduction of stomach cancer has been accompanied by increased incidence of colon cancer, and, on the basis of recent epidemiological findings, it is now recommended that we eat more traditional Japanese food.

Policy-oriented research of the kind exemplified by this *Monograph* tries to identify variables whose change is likely to solve or alleviate the targeted problem and that people will not mind changing. A good analogy is to a comparison of two societies or groups that differ in the incidence of beriberi, which would likely suggest the introduction of rice boiled with barley into the diet as a solution to its high incidence. The reduction of beriberi becomes possible with minimal sacrifice, and most people would be willing to accept that sacrifice because the benefit of reduction in incidence is far greater. Thus, if low mathematics achievement in the United States is like a high incidence of beriberi, then doing good policy-oriented research is easy, and recommendations based on such work can be straightforward.

However, if low mathematics achievement is like a high incidence of stomach cancer, then policy-oriented researchers must be much more cautious in designing studies, deriving conclusions, and making recommendations. Although a high incidence of such cancer is always a problem, it does not necessarily mean that a group characterized by low incidence is the healthier one—the low incidence of this form of disease may be accompanied by the high incidence of a different but equally serious illness. Moreover, attempts to decrease its incidence by manipulation of selected variables are likely to be difficult and, even if successful, may have negative side effects. Applied to policy-oriented research on mathematics achievement, the analogy indicates that we should examine two questions. Are the Asian countries really more successful in facilitating children's mathematical learning? Can the difference in mathematics achievement be reduced without undue sacrifice by changing the relevant sociocultural conditions of the United States to approximate those of the Asian countries?

There is no evidence in either this *Monograph* or the earlier publications of Stevenson et al. that the answer to the first question is affirmative. If the high mathematics achievement in the Asian countries primarily reflects understanding, then it indeed indicates superiority. However, if it is based mainly on skillful symbol manipulation, it must have inherent weaknesses. As Resnick (1987) put it, "Ordinary students are more likely to treat school mathematics as an invitation to master puzzle-like rule systems. Students who are good at such rule-learning . . . will perform quite well in school mathematics. But they will probably never love the subject, nor be very creative at it" (pp. 45–46). In other words, it is possible for high-achieving students not to experience the pleasure of understanding or even for them to hate mathematics.

In fact, this *Monograph* shows that the Japanese students in the follow-up had a stronger tendency to report that they were not good at mathematics than their American counterparts—in other words, to feel that mathematics was hard for them. I am personally afraid that Japanese students are paying a price for their high mathematics achievement. Using Resnick's (1987, p. 46) words, they are forced to "quickly discriminate among conditions of application" and "use effective strategies for rehearsal and practice" and thus cannot intrinsically "enjoy" mathematics. In any event, a more systematic comparison of the negative aspects of the learning of mathematics needs to be done in the future.

The answer to the second question also cannot be simply affirmative. If the high achievement among Asian students is accompanied by negative emotional reactions, then changing American sociocultural conditions to approximate those of the Asian countries will inevitably produce some of the same. Moreover, if my previous arguments are correct, changing American sociocultural conditions so as to improve children's mathematics achievement will be nearly impossible without posing a threat to cultural values: if American children's low mathematics achievement is generally a consequence of their cultural milieu—such as, for example, the availability of a broader range of possibilities and the encouragement to pursue whatever is individually more challenging—then it should be viewed as a part of the American culture. Since every culture has a more or less coherent matrix of values, policy-oriented researchers such as Stevenson et al. might consider carefully whether an intended change can be at all induced in the given matrix and whether doing so will not do harm to its coherence.

The great contribution of Stevenson and his associates is that they directed the attention of American researchers and of the American public to education in Asian countries and suggested ways for enhancing learning that had not been considered by other American investigators. However, I am a little worried that they sometimes idealize Japanese (and probably Chinese) sociocultural conditions for learning mathematics (and other subjects). To better our understanding across cultures, it is necessary to assess the weaknesses as well as the strengths of the Asian educational system.

References

Gagné, R. M. (1965). *The conditions of learning*. New York: Holt, Rinehart & Winston.

Goodnow, J. J. (in press). The socialization of cognition: Acquisition of cognitive values. *Human Development*.

Hatano, G. (1982a). Learning to add and subtract: A Japanese perspective. In T. P. Carpenter, J. M. Moser, & T. A. Romberg (Eds.), *Addition and subtraction: A cognitive perspective* (pp. 211–223). Hillsdale, NJ: Erlbaum.

Hatano, G. (1982b). Should parents be teachers too? A Japanese view. *Dokkyo University Bulletin of Liberal Arts*, **17**, 54–72.

Hatano, G. (1986). How do Japanese children learn to read: Orthographic and ecocultural variables. In B. Foorman and A. Siegel (Eds.), *Acquisition of reading skills: Cultural constraints and cognitive universals* (pp. 81–114). Hillsdale, NJ: Erlbaum.

Price, G. G., & Hatano, G. (in press). Toward a taxonomy of the roles home environments play in the formation of educationally significant individual differences. In S. Silvern (Ed.), *Literacy through family, community, and school interaction*. Greenwich, CT: JAI.

Resnick, L. B. (1987). Constructing knowledge in school. In L. S. Liben (Ed.), *Development and learning: Conflict or congruence?* (pp. 19–50). Hillsdale, NJ: Erlbaum.

Resnick, L. B. (1989). Developing mathematical knowledge. *American Psychologist*, **44**, 162–169.

Stigler, J. M., & Perry, M. (1988). Mathematics learning in Japanese, Chinese, and American classrooms. In G. Saxe & M. Gearhart (Eds.), *Children's mathematics* (pp. 27–54). San Francisco: Jossey-Bass.

REPLY

TO ACHIEVE

HAROLD W. STEVENSON AND SHIN-YING LEE

Comments by Giyoo Hatano, one of Asia's best-known researchers in the area of cognitive development, are always stimulating. We would like to take this opportunity, therefore, to respond to some of his interpretations about what we set out to do and some of his cautions and suggestions about what should be done next.

The impetus for the research discussed in the *Monograph* came from the domains of neither social policy nor mathematical cognition. Our original goal in undertaking this type of cross-cultural research was to study the role of orthography in reading. We were led into research on mathematics by the stunning differences we found in Asian and American children's mathematics achievement—differences that were evident in kindergarten and persisted through the elementary school years. Our goal in this *Monograph*, as Hatano correctly states at the beginning of his comments, was to attempt to describe how the differences in mathematics achievement are socioculturally produced. Only after finding these early differences in mathematics achievement have we had reason to try to analyze the mathematical knowledge of these particular groups of children in greater detail.

Symbols and Concepts?

We, like Hatano, realized that we would need a detailed profile of the competencies and weaknesses in mathematics before we could conclude that Chinese and Japanese children's excellence went beyond a solid knowledge of rules and routines. Although in this *Monograph* we report that they demonstrated superiority in solving word problems as well as in computation, demonstration of other types of superiority is also necessary.

We recently completed a study that provides such a demonstration. Hatano was not aware of its details, for the results are only now about to be published (Stevenson et al., in press; Stigler, Lee, & Stevenson, in press). We should mention this research, however, because the results provide a clear and direct response to one of the central deficiencies Hatanao found in the research reported in this *Monograph*: the issue of conceptual understanding versus symbol manipulation.

In our new study, we again evaluated children's skills in computation and solving word problems, but we also administered nine other tests. These tests covered the spectrum of knowledge and skills conveyed in elementary school mathematics classes as well as mathematics-related skills not directly taught in school. We relied on two sources of information in constructing the tests: the content of the children's mathematics textbooks and the opinions of mathematics educators. Some tests directly tapped what was in the textbooks; others required the application of this knowledge to novel problems.

Our battery included group tests of computation and geometry and individually administered tests of word problems, conceptual knowledge, operations, graphing, estimation, visualization, transformation of spatial relations, mental calculation, and speed of calculation. The computation test was given to nearly 7,200 first and fifth graders from a total of 20 schools in the Chicago metropolitan area and 31 schools in Sendai, Taipei, and Beijing. The individual tests were given to a subsample of 612 children (12 children from each grade in each school).

On every test, the average scores of the Chicago children fell below those of the Asian children. Asian superiority appeared in such diverse items as explaining to Martians about the ways in which addition could be used, deciding who won a race on the basis of information contained in a graph, determining the total amount of protein in different foods with specified amounts of protein, or making up their own word problems to fit a given mathematical formula. Answering items such as these requires more than the routine application of rules and procedures.

Children living in these Chinese and Japanese cities clearly outperformed American children in all areas of mathematics, whether the comparisons involved manipulation of symbols or demonstrating conceptual understanding, elite suburban American schools or schools in middle-class or inner-city neighborhoods. To answer Hatano's first major question, Yes, Asian countries—at least those that we have studied, along with Korea (Song & Ginsberg, 1987) and Hong Kong (McKnight et al., 1987)—really are more successful in facilitating children's mathematical learning.

These findings probably simplify the task of isolating the determinants of Asian superiority. Such general excellence must be derived from fundamental, pervasive characteristics of these cultures rather than from subtle differences that influence only certain skills. Some of these characteristics are discussed in this *Monograph*.

Cultural Impositions

There was ample evidence in our interviews and observations that Asian parents and teachers do value mathematics to a greater degree than do Americans. But excellence demands more than conveying the belief that something is important. Americans are enthusiastic about the importance of reading and accord it a dominant place in the elementary school curriculum. Even so, American children receive significantly lower scores in reading than do Chinese children from kindergarten through the elementary school years. These differences are not as dramatic as those in mathematics, but they also demand explanation. This is true, too, of science and geography, where American students also perform below the level of their peers in other industrialized countries. When we speak of deficiencies among American students, therefore, we cannot speak only of mathematics.

Hatano suggests that changing American sociocultural conditions so as to improve children's mathematical achievement will be nearly impossible without posing a threat to American values. An implication of this statement is that Americans would be wise to give up in mathematics and concentrate on other things in their culture. If mathematics were not such a fundamental subject, this might be worth discussing. But for any country to ignore the area of mathematics is to commit itself to a decline in science and technology, with an accompanying deterioration of its economy.

Asian Transplants

Cultures may not necessarily be benign or benevolent, but they are adaptive. Attempts to transplant characteristics of one culture to an alien culture always run the risk of systemic rejection. At the same time, the health of cultures, as is the case with individuals, can often be improved by observing other healthy systems and introducing appropriate adaptations. The Japanese have been outstandingly successful in doing this in many areas, including mathematics. In fact, the popular Japanese textbook series *Atarashii Sansu* (New mathematics) is an adaptation of many of the ideas from the New Math curriculum developed in the United States in the 1960s.

It seems doubtful that great cultural dislocations will necessarily follow as Americans reassess their emphasis on academic achievement, their involvement in their children's schooling, the realism of their self-evaluations, their standards for performance, or their emphasis on effort. Reassessment is a common prelude to innovation and change. Hatano's second major question, then, can be answered, Yes, it seems likely that American children's lower achievement in mathematics (as well as in reading, science, geography, and probably other subjects) can be reduced without undue sacrifice. Good teaching, interested parents, and hard work should enhance, rather than destroy, important elements in any culture and should improve rather than disturb the culture's coherence.

A pitfall may be encountered if the teaching is excessive, parents become too demanding, or work displaces other activities necessary for healthy development. Hatano implies that this is what has occurred in Asia. We often hear that this is the case in Japanese secondary schools (e.g., Rohlen, 1983), but neither we nor other writers have observed that this is typical during the elementary school years.

The Costs of Skill

Chinese and Japanese children may complain that mathematics is difficult, but this is a realistic assessment. Only the most exceptional students—especially during the elementary school years—prefer working so hard on a subject. What does Hatano propose? That children learn only what is intrinsically interesting to them? Few complex skills exist in which assiduousness and diligence are not major determinants of success. Does Hatano believe that the wide variety of options open to American children will lead to excellence in any of them? Does he really recommend an approach in which choice is made on the basis of ease and enjoyment rather than on the likelihood of beneficial outcomes? There are undoubtedly costs to Asian students in meeting the demands of their cultures, but there are also costs to the American students, as is evidenced in the high rates of illiteracy, school dropouts, and loss of opportunities for satisfying and challenging employment.

References

McKnight, C. C., Crosswhite, F. J., Dossey, J. A., Kifer, E., Swafford, J. O., Travers, K. J., & Cooney, T. J. (1987). *The underachieving curriculum: Assessing U.S. school mathematics from an international perspective.* Champaign, IL: Stipes.

Rohlen, T. (1983). *Japan's high schools.* Berkeley: University of California Press.

Song, M. J., & Ginsburg, H. P. (1987). The development of informal and formal mathematical thinking in Korean and U.S. children. *Child Development,* 58, 1286–1296.

Stevenson, H. W., Lee, S. Y., Chen, C., Lummis, M., Stigler, J. W., Liu, F., & Fang, G. (in press). Mathematics achievement of children in China and the United States. *Child Development.*

Stigler, J. W., Lee, S. Y., & Stevenson, H. W. (in press). Mathematical knowledge of Japanese, Chinese, and American children. *Monographs of the National Council for Teachers of Mathematics.*

CONTRIBUTORS

Harold W. Stevenson (Ph.D. 1951, Stanford University) is professor of psychology and fellow at the Center for Human Growth and Development at the University of Michigan, where he has been for the past 18 years. A graduate of the Naval Oriental Language School program in Japanese, he has had a long-term interest in Asia. He has been involved in cross-cultural studies in Japan, Taiwan, China, and Peru dealing with the influence of environmental factors and schooling on cognitive development and academic achievement.

Shin-ying Lee (Ph.D. 1987, University of Michigan) is research investigator at the University of Michigan. A graduate of National Taiwan University, she completed her doctoral dissertation on the attitudes and beliefs of Chinese mothers and children that are described in this *Monograph*. Currently, she is particularly interested in variables related to achievement motivation and in the instructional process in Chinese, Japanese, and American elementary school classrooms.

Chuansheng Chen is a doctoral candidate in developmental psychology at the University of Michigan. He attended Hangzhou University and Beijing Normal University before entering the University of Michigan. His special interest is in the study of the influences of family environments on cognitive development and the development of children's attitudes.

James W. Stigler (Ph.D. 1982, University of Michigan) is associate professor of psychology at the University of Chicago and holds appointments in the Departments of Psychology and Education and in the Center for Far Eastern Studies. Stigler's research centers on the investigation of quantitative and mathematical thinking. He is a 1989 recipient of the Boyd McCandless Award for young investigators in developmental psychology.

Chen-chin Hsu (M.D. 1951, National Taiwan University) is former director of the Children's Mental Health Center of the National Taiwan University Hospital and is currently superintendent of the National Cheng Gung University Hospital in Tainan, Taiwan. He received the Doctor of Medical Science degree from National Kobe Medical College and was a fellow in child psychiatry at Harvard University Medical School. He has conducted research on many aspects of child psychiatry and child development.

Seiro Kitamura (Ph.D. 1962, Tohoku University) was for many years affiliated with the Department of Psychology at Tohoku University as professor, chair, and editor of *Tohoku Psychologia Folia*. He is professor emeritus at Tohoku University and visiting professor at Tohoku Fukushi College. Kitamura is well known for his studies of personality and has published many books in this area, including *Psychology of the Self*.

Giyoo Hatano (Ph.D. 1966, University of Tokyo) is professor of psychology and cognitive science at Dokkyo University, Saitama, Japan. He is an associate editor of *Human Development* and an editorial board member of the *British Journal of Developmental Psychology, Cognition, Cognition and Instruction,* the *Journal of Mathematical Behavior,* the *Reading Research Quarterly,* and the *Newsletter of Laboratory of Comparative Human Cognition*. His theoretical and research interests are the interaction between everyday and school cognition, the social and motivational basis of understanding, and the reproduction and invention of knowledge in apprenticeship. His publications include "Two Courses of Expertise" (with Kayoko Inagaki), in *Child Development and Education in Japan,* ed. H. Stevenson, H. Azuma, and K. Hakuta (New York, 1986); "Social and Motivational Bases for Mathematical Understanding," in *Children's Mathematics,* ed. G. Saxe and M. Gearhart (San Francisco, 1988); and "Sharing Cognition through Collective Comprehension Activity" (with K. Inagaki), in *Socially Shared Cognition,* ed. L. Resnick and J. Levine (Washington, DC, in press).

STATEMENT OF EDITORIAL POLICY

The *Monographs* series is intended as an outlet for major reports of developmental research that generate authoritative new findings and use these to foster a fresh and/or better-integrated perspective on some conceptually significant issue or controversy. Submissions from programmatic research projects are particularly welcome; these may consist of individually or group-authored reports of findings from some single large-scale investigation or of a sequence of experiments centering on some particular question. Multiauthored sets of independent studies that center on the same underlying question can also be appropriate; a critical requirement in such instances is that the various authors address common issues and that the contribution arising from the set as a whole be both unique and substantial. In essence, irrespective of how it may be framed, any work that contributes significant data and/or extends developmental thinking will be taken under editorial consideration.

Submissions should contain a minimum of 80 manuscript pages (including tables and references); the upper limit of 150–175 pages is much more flexible (please submit four copies; a copy of every submission and associated correspondence is deposited eventually in the archives of the SRCD). Neither membership in the Society for Research in Child Development nor affiliation with the academic discipline of psychology are relevant; the significance of the work in extending developmental theory and in contributing new empirical information is by far the most crucial consideration. Because the aim of the series is not only to advance knowledge on specialized topics but also to enhance cross-fertilization among disciplines or subfields, it is important that the links between the specific issues under study and larger questions relating to developmental processes emerge as clearly to the general reader as to specialists on the given topic.

Potential authors who may be unsure whether the manuscript they are planning would make an appropriate submission are invited to draft an outline of what they propose and send it to the Editor for assessment.

This mechanism, as well as a more detailed description of all editorial policies, evaluation processes, and format requirements, is given in the "Guidelines for the Preparation of *Monographs* Submissions," which can be obtained by writing to Wanda C. Bronson, Institute of Human Development, 1203 Tolman Hall, University of California, Berkeley, CA 94720.